EVERGREENS

A Collection of Maine Outdoor Stories

JOHN HOLYOKE

Other Outdoor Books by Islandport Press

Making Tracks
By Matt Weber

Skiing with Henry Knox
By Sam Brakeley

Backtrack
By V. Paul Reynolds

Ghost Buck
By Dean Bennett

A Life Lived Outdoors
By George Smith

My Life in the Maine Woods
By Annette Jackson

Nine Mile Bridge
By Helen Hamlin

In Maine
By John N. Cole

Suddenly, the Cider Didn't Taste So Good
By John Ford

Leave Some for Seed
By Tom Hennessey

Birds of a Feather
By Paul J. Fournier

These and other Maine books available at
www.islandportpress.com

EVERGREENS

A Collection of Maine Outdoor Stories

JOHN HOLYOKE

ISLANDPORT PRESS

ISLANDPORT PRESS

Islandport Press
P.O. Box 10
Yarmouth, Maine 04096
www.islandportpress.com
info@islandportpress.com

First Islandport Printing, 2019

ISBN: 978-1-944762-77-3
ebook ISBN: 978-1-944762-85-8
Library of Congress Card Number: 2019931595
Printed in USA

Dean L. Lunt, Publisher
Book Design, Teresa Lagrange
Cover image courtesy of Gabor Degre, *Bangor Daily News*

For mom and dad, who always listened to the stories I told,
even when they'd already heard them a dozen times before.

TABLE OF CONTENTS

Author's Note

All of us writers, I'd bet, have one thing in common. Or maybe two. First, many of us began playing with words because we quickly learned that typically in writing, there were few pesky math problems. And second, most every writer will tell you, "Why yes, of course I've got a book in me … somewhere … somehow."

Yes, we're all would-be novelists just searching for the perfect story to tell. Me? My great American novel is currently in a cardboard box awaiting a long-overdue and much-needed edit. But it's there. I can honestly tell my friends that I've completed a novel, even if none of them have ever read it.

The work in front of you, you may have guessed, is not that novel. Instead, it's a collection of stories—all of them true, I swear!—that I've told *Bangor Daily News* readers over the past eighteen years or so. And the reason it's now in your hands is pretty simple—back in 2017, I finally figured out that some magical, mythical publisher was not going to cold-call me and ask if I had a book to sell. Instead, with a couple decades of "chapters" at my disposal, I decided to make the cold call myself, to see how the publishing biz works, and to find out if there was a spot in it for me.

My first stop was Islandport Press, at a seminar for aspiring authors that the company held at their Yarmouth headquarters. What I learned over the course of a few hours would fill pages (and trust me, I kept pretty good notes), but I won't re-teach those lessons here. Instead, I'll share the *Eureka* moment that I experienced that cold autumn evening in a room filled with people a lot like me, who value the written word and love having a good book in their hands.

"We tell stories," Islandport boss Dean Lunt told us that night, sharing the company's mission. I immediately started smiling, and figured that I'd found an appropriate outlet for the book that's in your hands today, even though I'd not yet prepared that book for submission.

The reason for my grin? That's exactly how I've been describing myself for more than twenty years—I tell stories, too. Whether I've been officially described as a reporter, columnist, sportswriter, feature writer, or book reviewer, all roles that I've played, one thing has remained true in my mind—I'm a storyteller.

As such, I'm here to take you on an adventure. Along the way, you're welcome to laugh or cry or smile or reach for the phone to tell an old friend they still matter. All are suitable reactions. The title, *Evergreens*, is a nod to my journalism background and is a term that refers to stories that have no shelf life, like the ones you'll find in this book. In reading through them while preparing this book, I thought they resonate as well now as they did when they were written.

Included you'll find several dozen stories I've shared with loyal readers. For me, it turns out, the book was always a work in progress, one column, or feature, or chapter at a time. I didn't think of those pieces as parts of a whole at the time, but now, looking back at some of that work, I think it works well as a package.

The stars of this show, it should be stated, are pretty easy to identify. First, Maine's people are special, and those who've shared their tales with me have made my job more enjoyable than you can imagine. And second, the state of Maine, itself, for giving writers like me the chance to venture out into some magical places in search of stories.

There are more complete acknowledgements at the end of this book, but up front, I've got to say thanks to my friends, for letting me share some of their secrets. Thanks also to the strangers who welcomed me into their homes and hunting camps.

Thanks to my wife, Karen, for understanding the odd hours of the job, encouraging me to chase these tales, and for listening to me as I tell her the same story for the umpteenth time. Yes, it's fun to be the storyteller. But to be the storyteller's wife? That takes more than a fair bit of patience, and I try hard not to forget that fact.

So go forth, and read a tale or two before you turn in. This collection works best if consumed in front of a cozy wood stove with a friendly pooch at your feet, but that isn't a requirement. Enjoy.

Then, do me a favor: The next time you end up on the receiving part of a tale you think I might enjoy, drop me a line. (I'm really not too hard to track down. Then, who knows? You might even end up in your own "chapter" in another book, if that ever comes to pass.

See you on the trails.

John Holyoke
Brewer, Maine
October 2019

John Holyoke with some bear cubs. Photo by Gabor Degre, Bangor Daily News.

Foreword

There is nothing John Holyoke enjoys more than telling a good story. And he has stockpiled a sizeable repertoire over the years. It's a talent he acquired from his late father, Vaughn Holyoke, a man who extolled the virtues of hard work and love for family while building lasting relationships with friends and acquaintances encountered during his extensive travels around the state.

In his first book, *Evergreens*, John Holyoke shares a special collection of his favorite newspaper columns from his first seventeen years as an outdoors writer and columnist for the *Bangor Daily News*. He tells relatable tales of people who passionately pursue outdoor activities in some of Maine's most beautiful and far-flung places. He also sprinkles in personal recollections of memorable events that helped shape his outlook on the benefits of spending time with friends and acquaintances visiting the state's woods, fields, and waters.

Holyoke's ability to build a sense of trust with Mainers enables him to generate personal, heartfelt accounts that convey a true sense of what makes living and playing in the Maine outdoors so special. That includes encounters with countless creatures, both wild and domesticated, that have both fascinated and confounded him.

In *Evergreens*, Holyoke and friends cross paths with salmon, brook trout, deer, dogs, turkeys, moose, hamsters, "river vultures," frogs, and squirrels. There are moments both poignant and silly, but it is his curiosity, compassion, and honesty in sharing stories of Maine people, some of whom have endured difficult circumstances, that enable his columns to touch the heart of readers.

Holyoke conveys to readers his passion for enjoying Maine's outdoor pursuits, when spending time with a fly rod in hand or a shotgun slung over his shoulder. The stories in *Evergreens* include time spent afield with many memorable characters.

Holyoke's approach, whether pursuing his own outdoor adventures or telling the compelling stories of others, is simple—he strives to live and learn, to laugh and love, to eat well—and maybe even to shed a few tears. Most importantly, he tries to enjoy the moment and help elicit some of those feelings from his readers.

So, throw a couple of pieces of wood into the stove or fireplace and settle into your favorite chair with *Evergreens* and enjoy Holyoke's superb storytelling. The stories are crafted with an emphasis on sharing what makes living and playing in the Maine outdoors so special to so many.

Pete Warner
Digital Sports Editor
Bangor Daily News, August 2019

EVERGREENS

A Collection of Maine Outdoor Stories

The Brook

As trout streams go, the site of my earliest fishing excursions was nothing special, if, that is, it can truly be said that any trout stream is "nothing special." What I mean is that this particular stream wasn't spectacular in any way, nor that much different from other tiny eastern Maine streams in the 1970s.

The stream was narrow. It was shallow. Several times a summer, after we had climbed every tree we could climb, were unable to settle our latest croquet rules dispute, and were waterlogged by swimming for hours, we'd head to the stream. Rods in hand. Worms safely stored in the nifty, twist-to-open dispenser (the odd slogan, "Half a turn, there's your worm," still resonates, thirty years later).

The brook must have had a name, although that official label, whatever it was, never mattered much to us. To my brother and sister and me, it was just "The Brook." Our frequent summer adventures always began just upstream from the lake at a place we still called "Bumpy Bridge," although the old log structure that earned it the name has long since been replaced.

One of my favorite Maine guides often says that on his chosen river, there are certain special places that he won't abandon until his sport has caught a fish.

"There are always fish there," he'll say. "If we don't catch one, it means we're going to have a bad trip."

To us, Bumpy Bridge was just such a spot. Every adventure began there, with the three of us hand-lining our worms between the logs of the seldom-used bridge. We'd lie on our bellies, peer through the cracks, and wait for the telltale tug. The fish couldn't see us that way, we figured and although the gaps between the logs weren't too wide, neither were the tiny trout we were hiding from. Eventually, however, we always moved on. The Brook awaited. And so did the trout. Maybe.

The ultimate goal, I realize now, was never "to catch fish." Not really. Surely we intended to do so, and most days, we succeeded. But it seems what we really wanted to do was simpler, more elemental, more primitive—we just wanted to go somewhere we hadn't been before.

On a small brook like ours, doing that meant bushwhacking farther upstream than we'd ever bushwhacked before. Some days, we simply ran out of time (or caught too many fish on our way upstream) to do so. But other days, we'd hop rocks, climb steep embankments, and fish our way deeper and deeper into the woods. On those days, we'd round one final corner, spy an unfamiliar (and therefore, in the eyes of a ten-year-old, undiscovered) pool and smile.

Progress was incremental, of course. Despite our best-laid plans to really, truly explore the entire brook, our jaunts could only be as long as our meal schedules allowed. Our best trips began shortly after lunch, but we always knew they had to finish before supper, no matter what—Mom's rule—and Mom's rules were not to be trifled with.

Eventually, we figured, we would trek The Brook in its entirety. We would need to start early. Fish less. Hike more. Eventually, we would discover where this little trickle originated. On those days we actually worked our way deep into the woods, days when every twist and turn along the Brook unveiled new fishing grounds, were rare (the farther you head afield, I have since learned, the more advance planning is necessary). But those days were also the most memorable. Deep in the woods, things were different. Out there, there were bears and all sorts of unknown critters looking for a tasty and tender ten-year-old snack (or so we told each other). When deep in the woods, we young adventurers tended to fish pools closer to each other and to look over our shoulders a bit more often.

My cousin, always a bit more adventurous than the rest of us, came prepared. He carried a knife, though I never found out whether it was really a fishing knife or actually a self-defense, bear-fighting knife, as he may have led us to believe. During one deep-woods snack break, he stuck his knife in a log for safekeeping, and forgot all about it until we arrived back at camp hours later. For a few days, I searched for his prized possession and learned an important wilderness truth—in the woods, one log looks much like another, even the rotten, knife-holding logs.

Years later, I found that knife. It was a rusted, forgotten relic left by a boy who had moved on to bigger and theoretically better things. Eventually, each of us did the same thing. We moved on. We stopped fishing at Bumpy Bridge. We stopped hiking upstream. And I suppose some of us even stopped wondering where The Brook originated and whether we'd ever get there.

A few years ago, I returned to Bumpy Bridge. There were no logs to peer between, nor any eager adventurers fishing the shallow water.

Farther upstream, I found, there are homes. Culverts scar the once-pristine trickle. The wilderness paradise of our childhood is no more, it seems.

Now, years later, I still don't know what The Brook's real name is and I still haven't hiked to its source. But even though the waters I fish now are typically bigger and more spectacular, I've come to realize that I haven't completely moved on after all.

Not really.

The mysteries of that childhood trout stream are strong, you see. And the memories of those hot summer days keep me thinking about the places we loved so much and wondering about the places we never quite discovered.

Camp and Camping

My parents were smart, hardworking people. Shortly after they married they made a decision that would shape all of our lives—they bought land on Beech Hill Pond in Otis and built a camp at which we'd spend countless summer days. Many Mainers grew up the same way, heading to camp on weekends or on vacations, where they'd swim, fish, climb trees, and relax.

This first section of essays contains some stories about camps, and some other pieces that deal with the joys (and potential pitfalls) of camping—actually getting out there, pitching a tent, and sleeping among the bears … and moose … and raccoons. So sit back and enjoy a few tales. I bet you'll find a few that resonate with you. And for your sake, I hope the column about bees doesn't bring back any bad memories for you.

1. Cross Country Croquet

On a brilliantly sunny Sunday, I headed to the family camp on Beech Hill Pond, disembarked from my truck, and was approached by a wiry teen carrying a wooden hammer.

"It just got mowed this morning," he said, cryptically, peeking over his shoulder at a pack of hammer-wielding buddies. "Course is running fast. Hard to hold on the bank."

"What about that sidehill?" I asked. "That's nasty."

"Not as bad going down as coming back," he said.

I nodded, understanding the jargon in a way only veterans of our hardscrabble sport truly can. If, that is, any of us truly understand our own hardscrabble sport entirely.

At some camps, people gather for games of horseshoes. At others, they splash in the water, or throw Frisbees. For years, "The Game" at our camp has been cross country croquet.

During a quick Internet search, I learned that croquet "has a reputation for being a genteel game." Perhaps that's why my nephew, Kyle, refuses to call our version of the game "croquet," and deliberately mispronounces it "crow-kett" when he's trying to round up players for a game.

This game is not genteel.

It is not relaxed.

And it is not, purists would likely point out, a game that resembles proper croquet in the least. All of which is perfectly fine with us.

We do not honor the United States Croquet Association requirement of white attire (Heck, if most male participants are even wearing shirts, it'd be surprising). Not that our game doesn't enjoy some grand tradition of its own, of course.

Our game is probably similar to that played at camps around the state. In its present form, our version began some twenty-five years ago, when a bunch of bored college students (my brother Glen seems to have been the ringleader) were looking for a way to kill time between beers while spending a weekend at camp. They grabbed an all-but-forgotten croquet set and a few bent-beyond-recognition wickets, walked around the lawn, and began formulating their sport.

It didn't take long before they began tinkering with the game and adopting rules that carry through to this day. These rules have been handed down from the ringleader to his sons, nephew, and niece. They have in turn been handed down to friends of those sons, who show up many weekends to play a game or six.

Since its origin in the 1980s, we've broken mallets, lost balls, bent wickets, and worn out several croquet sets, all in the pursuit of that grand tradition. The most important part of our game, you quickly find out, is that as soon as you think you've got it figured out, you're wrong.

Man, are you wrong.

It is, after all, "cross country" croquet. And all it takes to make the game even more interesting is another nephew, or son, or assorted pal deciding it's his turn to set the wickets in the most devious places he can think of.

Ah, yes. Setting the wickets.

Real croquet (as far as I've been able to ascertain) relies on a predetermined course, with wickets in the same places, day after day after day. The grass is smooth. The balls roll true. Birds chirp happily. Everyone has fun. Nobody throws their mallet into the woods and leaves the course, crying.

That's not our game.

Cross country croquet is much more fluid than that (and when I say fluid, I not only mean it changes, I also mean it's likely you'll end up playing a ball out of the lake at some point). The course architect has the ultimate power (although he can be shouted down by the masses if a potential wicket placement seems particularly dastardly).

Side-hill wickets are common. In some years, wickets have been put up against rocks, or behind trees, or on top of rotting stumps. That day's course architect would surely admit that stump-wickets are an exceedingly bad idea, and break a general rule: Hard is good. Tricky is good. Impossible is not good.

The field of play is not a field at all. It's a lawn (in places). It's a sunbathing area (in others). It's the woods (if you're unlucky). And it's the water (if you're not careful). Some wickets are placed in shaggy grass. Others are placed on the dead patch of former lawn where my boat lay all winter and most of the spring. (Note to players: That territory is greasy-fast. Picture Augusta National's greens, without the grass, and with a four-mile-long water hazard lurking, ready to gobble up errant shots.)

Golf has hazards. Our game does, too, except they're not really planned.

The grill always stands in the same place, over near the horseshoe pit—it will remain there. You can not move it. Ever. When a ball rolls under this grill-hazard, the player must lie down on his or her belly and poke it back into play (unless it's nearly suppertime and the grill has been lit, at which time the rules committee might show a bit of lenience. Then again, it might not).

The hammock is also in play. Even if someone's lying in it. You are not allowed to hit the slumbering sunbather with a mallet to get them to move out of your way.

Come to think of it, we may have a few genteel traditions after all. A few. Not many.

Cross country croquet is a rough game. Well, now it is, again. There was that span of years when the nephews and niece were young—let's call it the "dead ball era"—when the rules committee decided that whacking a seven-year-old's croquet ball into the forest and making them play it as it lies might be a bit extreme.

Now, thankfully, everyone has grown up a bit, and we can again start acting like children. "Sending" players into the woods or into the lake (just place your ball next to theirs, step on yours, aim, and swing as hard as you possibly can) has regained its strategic importance. Even if it makes no strategic sense, it's an immensely satisfying option to consider when you're losing.

A quick note: Those players (like me) who enjoy sending their rivals into the puckerbrush are easy to spot. They're the ones walking around wearing a single shoe, so that they don't break their foot when they start flailing wildly at a ball they're standing on.

In real croquet, I've learned, players are allowed to carry a ball back onto the field of play and place it in-bounds after they've been banished to the hinterlands by a rival. Not in our game. There is no out-of-bounds. The forest is in play. Stop whining. Go find your ball. We'll see you in a half hour.

In our game, sticks and dead branches can be moved. Spectators and beach toys can't. When the game starts, everything that's lying around (whether an inner tube or lawn chair or a person) becomes part of the course. No drops. No lifts. No relief. No griping.

There are, of course, exceptions.

My brother and the founding fathers of our great game saw to that. For instance, there's the soggy-ball amendment to the whack-'em-into-the-woods rule. The founding fathers quickly learned that getting back onto the field of play from the woods wasn't too difficult—usually. It might take you a few turns to get back to civilization, but you'd eventually return.

The lake, however, was another matter.

Competitors who found themselves in the water (down a steep, rocky embankment) often spent the rest of the game there, trying to smack a floating croquet ball out of its soggy lie. Nowadays, thanks to the rule-makers, a player can skip a turn, retrieve his ball from the lake, and place it on terra firma.

Real croquet players are expected to behave nicely toward their rivals. No trash talking. No distracting. No funny business whatsoever. In our game, I'm sure you've already guessed, such rules do not exist. Heckling happens (especially when I'm playing). So do distractions. And funny business? Well, those of us who aren't particularly good at hitting balls through wickets get to be quite proficient at the more subtle ways of gaining an advantage.

And in our game, we'd have it no other way.

2. Hooking Up Camp Water

Each summer, thousands of Mainers head to their seasonal camps, where they'll eventually be joined by friends and relatives eager to have a bit of fun in the sun.

Eventually.

First, of course, camp owners must make sure everything's ship-shape after another harsh Maine winter. They clean. They tidy. They chase down bats, sweep up ants, and set traps to capture the mouse herd.

Many undertake one of the most puzzling, perturbing, perplexing chores of all. They turn into amateur plumbers. "Putting the water in" is one of those honored Maine traditions that doesn't get written about often, to be honest. The reason is simple—it's difficult to wax poetic about the camp record fourteen swear words Uncle Timmy strung together when the pump spit in his face for the seventh time in five minutes.

In most cases, putting the water in is merely frustrating. In some cases, it can be downright dangerous.

Take my buddy's camp, for instance. A few years back, I helped him put his water in (which means I stood around and tried to stay out of the way). He quickly learned the pump house was occupied—by bees. And it quickly became apparent those bees didn't like sharing space with our intrepid plumber.

He squealed and scrambled out of the cave-like shack. I yelled angrily at the bees, because if I hadn't, my buddy would have heard me laughing.

Yes, "putting the water in" is unappreciated. But every spring, it provides some of the most hilarious highlights of the season—as long as you're not the one the pump is spitting at.

And I'm not. Not yet.

At our camp, as of yesterday, that job still belongs to my dad. He's the one who knows which holes to plug, and which tools work best, and how to get the pump to stop humming and wheezing, and to start pumping.

My brother, Glen, and I? Well, we're the ones who wade into the chilly lake, anchoring the intake pipe as we go. That sounds like rough duty . . . up until the pump starts spitting.

Over the years, we've learned a few things about putting the water in, my brother and I. First: Stand behind someone. The pump will begin to belch pressurized water at some point (usually when Dad's face is right next to the belch-hole). Our job (as far as we've been able to figure) is to stand far away from the action to stay dry, but close enough so that our chuckles are barely audible. (Note to Dad: You didn't hear this from me, but it was Glen's idea.)

Second: Figure out which tool Dad wants by the way he holds his hands, and how loud he grunts (even if his mouth is full of belch-water).

Third: Don't expect the pump to actually work until Dad has said a naughty word. Or two.

Fourth: If something breaks, or someone begins bleeding, don't make a peep. Not a peep.

Laughing at a perpetually uncooperative pump is acceptable, we've learned. Laughing at a broken one (or an injured amateur plumber) will not be forgiven nearly as easily.

And next year, that unforgiving amateur plumber might decide that priming the pump (and spending too much time looking down the barrel of the belch-hole) is someone else's job.

3. Camping With Kids Can Be an Adventure

After several weeks of talking and planning and (this is the critical part) praying for good weather, my party of intrepid campers loaded up and hit the road Friday for a hopefully memorable weekend. Check that. We actually hoped it would be an enjoyable weekend. Memorable, I have found, is a gate that swings both ways.

This excursion was a special one—the first taken together with my girlfriend and her three young children—and we were determined to make it as memorable, or I should say enjoyable, as we could.

Two cars. Two adults. Three children (a seven-year-old boy and five-year-old twins, one of each gender). More than enough gear and

Evan O'Kresik and Ava O'Kresik enjoy s'mores while camping with their parents. Photo by Linda Coan O'Kresik, Bangor Daily News.

food. And a master plan. That, we figured, would be plenty. It didn't take long for the master plan to begin fraying.

"It's clearing to the north," I said when we stopped in Dover-Foxcroft, in part to feed the troops, and in part so that we could stop the same troops from paying attention to the impressive thunderstorm we'd been driving through.

It was, in fact, clearing to the north. And we were, in fact, heading north. When we checked in at scenic Lily Bay State Park, the rain was over (or so we told each other). The mosquitoes were fierce, but expected. The weekend would be wonderful. No doubt about it.

Then we began unpacking gear, lugging it down a mucky path to our campsite, and setting up camp. By the time we had the tent out of its bag, it was sprinkling again. By the time I had decided which poles were which, it was raining. And by the time we had begun actually assembling our shelter, it was pouring.

"I'm wet," one twin complained.

"I'm cold," screamed the other.

"It's raining," a third helpful voice chimed in.

They were right. It was wet . . . and cold . . . and raining.

And we were stuck in it.

Before long (but not before the ruckus roused otherwise peaceful red squirrels and raccoons, I'm sure), we had ourselves a tent. A soggy, muddy, wilting tent, but a tent nonetheless.

Karen took charge from there, marching her soggy children inside, toweling them off, tucking them into pajamas, and telling them to pile onto a single air mattress to avoid larger puddles.

Outside, I walked around in the mud, pulling ropes, sinking pegs, and trying to remember how easy this seemed when we had done our test run two days earlier in the sunshine.

I stood outside and pulled more ropes and sank more pegs, not that I was intentionally avoiding the in-tent melee. I just figured that our situation called for a sensible division of labor. And I was perfectly happy to labor outside. In the rain. In the dark.

Before long (but not before I imagined that we were close to being evicted from the campground) all three children fell asleep. The rain had stopped. And Karen told me a secret. One of our air mattresses was not holding air.

"But the kids are sleeping great," I told her.

"That's because they're not sleeping on the one that doesn't hold air," she told me.

As a forty-three-year-old single man with no children of his own, it took me a minute to realize the gravity of that statement.

I tried to explain that kids could sleep on anything, even rocks, and wake up fresh as daisies. I tried to explain that if we were sneaky, we could let the twins fall asleep on their air mattress, then transfer them to the equally comfy ground. We might even pass it off as a camping tradition, if they complained. I then tried to explain that I was just kidding about those two options. But through it all, both she and I realized one thing—we were going to sleep on the cold, hard ground.

The next morning, a bright-eyed seven-year-old greeted me at the picnic table.

"How did you sleep?" he asked happily, munching a Pop Tart, the previous night's deluge forgotten.

I won't share my reply.

Regardless, there's no sense in dwelling on bad things when you're camping. That's what I'd told the kids. That's what I believed myself. And that's what we did. Even if it rained. Even if two of us were sleeping on an airless mattress.

On what turned into a busy Saturday, the kids swam in chilly Moosehead Lake, and played on a path that ran from our campsite to the water's edge. We tried our hand at fishing for bass off the nearby docks, but had little luck. I explained that the fish we were targeting had met people before, and knew how to avoid being caught. (I didn't reveal that I just don't catch many fish, regardless of how educated the bass are).

We drove to Elephant Mountain and hiked into the site where a B-52 crashed in 1963. All three children were interested, amazed, and appropriately respectful of the scene. We then visited my sister and her family and had a cookout.

Later, we saw a rabbit (to go with a moose we'd spotted on the drive up, and a couple of red squirrels). And after a brief sun shower, we saw a beautiful rainbow. Prompted by the twins, we began discussing ways to spend the imaginary loot that we would be able to split should we ever find that pot of gold at the end of a rainbow.

Eventually, we settled in for a evening in front of a campfire, turning marshmallows and chocolate into s'mores and gobbling them down. Later still, Karen and I sat by the fire listening to the light snores drifting out from the tent. A raccoon stopped to survey our trash bag, then our picnic table, then tried to run off into the woods with an uncooked tin of Jiffy Pop.

The raccoon, a large, fluffy fellow, surely meant business, and he didn't leave for good until we hid all of our edibles in the car. And then it was time for bed again.

"About that air mattress," I said, reviewing our options.

Karen smiled, but assured me that we ought to let the children have the best beds again. That sounded good to me, and before long, I was sleeping on the cold, hard ground, perfectly content. That is, I thought I was content.

When I woke in the morning, shoulders and hips and back stiff, I rethought that contentedness. And when I opened one eye, I forgot all about it.

There, just a few feet away, sharing my cold, hard ground, was a slumbering five-year-old. And there, high and dry on the plush, bouncy air mattress, was Karen. *Traitor*, I thought.

Eventually, a slightly plausible explanation emerged. It seems (or so Karen says) that all night long, children kept rolling off the air mattress and landing on her. It seems (or so Karen says) that at 5 a.m., she simply decided to stop fighting gravity and swapped places with one tumbling twin. And it seems (or so Karen says) that's where I discovered them less than one hour later.

At first, I shook my head in mock consternation. I stopped that, because it made my already sore neck hurt even worse. Then I started to chuckle. A few hours later, I realized something important. We had succeeded in our quest.

Our first camping excursion together had been an enjoyable one. And it had been equally memorable.

4. Time Heals Old Camping Wounds

When camping with small children, it's only natural to wish for the impossible—a carefree trip during which bugs don't bite, nobody bleeds, and you are never, ever forced to set up camp in a rainstorm.

A year earlier, when I embarked on just such an adventure to Lily Bay State Park, none of those things happened. Well, maybe one did. I can't recall anybody actually bleeding (but it was raining so hard, I'm not sure I would have noticed).

Fishing on the East Outlet of the Kennebec River. Photo by Linda Coan O'Kresik, Bangor Daily News.

Still, there were enough pitfalls (have I mentioned the rainstorm, and the resulting mud?) that I spent much of those camping excursions asking myself a very basic question: How are we ever going to convince the kids to go camping again?

Thankfully, it seems time is the ultimate healer of bug bites, soggy drawers, and unpleasant memories. On the way back from tee ball Sunday, one six-year-old camper asked me a typical six-year-old question. Read that: There was no preface and it made little sense at first.

"Remember the plane crash, where only a few people survived?" he asked.

After drawing upon my professional journalist skills and quizzing him for a bit, I finally figured out what we were chatting about. He had not been watching the world news when I thought he'd been watching SpongeBob. Phew. He was talking about the B-52 crash on

Elephant Mountain, not far from Greenville. We had hiked to the site the previous summer, after the rain fell and the bugs began biting.

"Can we go there again, if we go camping?" he asked.

Although I finished that weekend believing that our foray into camping had been a success, I wasn't quite sure.

Maybe they'd only remember the rain. Maybe they'd only remember the bugs. Maybe they had bled, and I was too busy hiding from the rain and the bugs to notice. Maybe (*gulp*) they hadn't had any fun at all.

Now, out of the blue, one young camper wanted to talk about heading into the woods again. And he was smiling.

"Remember the egg-in-a-bag?" he asked, referring to one morning's kid-friendly breakfast.

"I do," I told him.

"I want that again," he said.

Then, after a brief pause, he asked the big question.

"Can we go camping again?"

I think you all know the answer to that one.

5. The Everything Box

Organization, I am told, is key to a successful camping trip. Take only what you need and leave the other stuff home. And, most importantly, know where you put the stuff you need, so you can find it when you need it. I have listened closely to experienced campers. I have worked hard on my organizational skills. And still, I learn (at the worst possible times) there are holes in my master plan.

Over the weekend, I embarked on a fun-filled camping trip to Lamoine State Park, with Karen and her three children.

The weather cooperated (except for that monstrous thunderstorm that ripped through on Friday night). The bugs cooperated (except for the bees that kept buzzing around our fruit juice). The tent cooperated (after I realized that I'd forgotten how to set it up, and again reread the tattered directions).

The firewood even cooperated, and when a Cub Scout dropout (me) is in charge of fire-building, that's always a development worth celebrating.

Lamoine State Park, if you haven't visited, is a real gem. It sits on Frenchman Bay, and the views are breathtaking. Seven-year-old Gordon thought the park's treehouse and playground were more breathtaking; to each his own.

All in all, the trip was a fantastic success; at least as far as the kids knew. They were too busy dodging bees and talking about the treehouse to realize that my organizational skills left a bit to be desired.

Let me be perfectly clear here: I tried. I really tried. But somehow, my plan came unfurled at about the time we opened up the tote I call The Everything Box.

While packing for trips, I take special care to put all our necessities in obvious places. We have a dry box that holds everything from paper towels to graham crackers. If it doesn't need to stay cold, and it's not a permanent camping supply (such as mantles for the Coleman lantern, let's say), it goes in the dry box.

I have a cooler for perishables. I have a not-so-cooler, which just doesn't insulate too well, but will keep chocolate bars and fruit from melting or spoiling if we're careful not to open it too much.

And then there's The Everything Box.

That's the mother of boxes. It holds all the stuff that I only need when I'm camping. Like tongs and a spatula and a frying pan. Like mantles for the lantern and matches to light the lantern and a funnel to put fuel in the stove.

It has everything. Everything Box. Get it?

Unfortunately, someone has been pirating items from The Everything Box since I last used it two summers ago.

Someone had to find matches to light the grill, and never put them back. Someone took out the tongs to flip a steak, and never put them back. Someone used the last mantles . . . and never bought new ones.

I have a good idea who the culprit is, but I'll take the fifth to avoid self-incrimination.

In any case, after two years of picking and pirating, The Everything Box morphed into The Where's Everything? Box. Unfortunately, I didn't find that out until suppertime on Saturday, when the kids' foil-packet meals (choose your favorite ingredients, make your own, toss 'em onto the campfire coals) were simmering . . . and bubbling . . . and nearly burning.

The tool I'd need to extract those little tinfoil-wrapped delicacies was right where I'd left it: In The Everything Box. Or maybe it wasn't.

I needed tongs, but they were gone. I needed a spatula, but it was missing. I needed something, anything, that could rescue those little foil packets before supper was ruined. And luckily, I had just what I needed.

Karen.

As the tinfoil began to blacken and my rescue maneuvers failed (ever try to pick up a meal with nothing but your fire-poking stick?), Karen stepped into the fray, moved me aside, and got to work. Two pieces of firewood became oversized chopsticks (she's good with chopsticks). Karen deftly lifted each meal from the inferno. I couldn't have done better with tongs and a spatula, if I'd had them.

Supper was saved. The trip was salvaged. Children ate their foil-wrapped creations, then asked for seconds. Everything was perfect. No thanks to me, or my still-developing organizational skills, of course.

But there's always next time.

6. Spring Solitude at Camp

For years, "camp" has existed as a strictly seasonal retreat, with all the attendant perks, and a few quirks. The lake, our own personal swimming pool and playground, is just yards away, but some nights, when the warm summer breeze isn't blowing, it seems possible the blackflies might swoop in and carry you back to their lair.

Our camp is cozy—until nighttime, when everyone heads inside. At that point, even the most nostalgic among us admits that "cozy" gives way to "crowded."

The camp is uninsulated, and even a moderate summer shower drums on the roof, creating that rustically unique cacophony that never sounds quite the same when you're not in the woods. Of course, without insulation, you're always at the whim of the weather, whether that weather is hot or cold, dry or humid.

For three months or so each year, camp has been a haven from the city heat, a place to gather with family and friends, and to enjoy our special spot in the Maine woods. Forget the fact that as time passes, camp doesn't seem nearly as far off the beaten path as it once did. It's still camp.

At least, in the summer it will be.

But I've learned over the past few weeks, after moving temporarily to this lake during the pre-summer chill of May, my nostalgic view of camp isn't entirely accurate. Not that that's necessarily a bad thing, mind you.

It's just that those lazy, hazy summer days that remain perfectly etched in my mind's eye are special in a way I hadn't really noticed. Spending time alone at camp is at once invigorating and humbling. The air does smell different there. I notice birds singing, and try to catalogue every creak, snap, and bump in the night. But this is not the camp I grew up loving. Not really.

It is still special. It's still a haven. But in the weeks before the lake truly awakes from its winter slumber, before the weekend-only neighbors return, and before any but the most hardy swimmers dare leap off their docks, it's decidedly different.

Things move slowly now, even more slowly than on those lazy, hazy days I remember so well. And while the theory of "solitude" is pretty soothing, the reality can be something else entirely.

Those paddles down the lake are still interesting—the bald eagle that joined me on Memorial Day weekend was particularly surprising, as I'd never seen one on the lake in more than forty years of visiting camp.

I'm seeing more wildlife on my drives to and from work (or, perhaps, I'm just noticing the wildlife that's always been there)—a young moose, a deer, two rabbits, several squirrels, a sizeable flock of speedy wild turkeys, and a hairy, low-slung beast of unknown origin that I'd really like to get a second peek at.

My memories of camp are not filled with hours of solitary sitting, reading, pondering, and fly-tying, you see. I don't remember many solo paddles down the lake's shoreline, nor many minutes spent entirely alone in the place my father and his brother built years ago.

Instead, I remember the *people* I shared those paddles with, the people I dragged behind the boat on a tube, the people I shared my small fishing boat with as we tried to trick a togue or two on a balmy August afternoon.

I don't remember sitting in front of a raging fire alone; I remember the stories told around those fires and the laughter from those illuminated by its glowing embers.

I remember climbing trees with my brother, playing cross-country croquet with my nephews and niece, and tossing horseshoes with anyone who'd play (and put up with my non-stop chatter).

I remember complaining to others about the personal watercraft that buzz too close to shore, or buzz around in circles, or buzz back and forth (or, on those rare days when they're not buzzing, I remember complaining about the way they buzzed the day before).

I remember marching down the camp road to our trout stream. We always wanted to find out where that brook came from, and we're all still wondering, years after we last headed upstream, happily hopping from rock to rock.

A little bit of solitude can do a man good. At least, that's what people tell me.

But on cold May nights in that uninsulated camp, I found myself more than willing to give up a bit of that solitude. I found myself sitting by the fire, lost in those memories, eagerly waiting for those lazy, hazy, busy days to return.

And they will return. Of that, I'm sure. That happens when summer truly arrives, when the kids get out of school and when the weekend-only neighbors head back to their own special places in the Maine woods. This year, when all that happens, I don't think I'll mind all that much.

That is, after all, what camp's all about . . . at least in the mind's eye of one solitary man.

7. Junkapork

As rocks go, ours is neither majestic nor monstrous. It doesn't strike fear into those who clamber up it, and rarely reduces its guests to trembling wrecks as they perch on the edge, just a hop away from the cool waters below.

No, our rock is neither as fearsome as some, nor as dangerous as others. It is small. It is safe. For generations of campers at Beech Hill Pond, it is our rock. And without it, camp life wouldn't be quite the same.

Many of the state's lakes are dotted with similar rocks, thanks to the glaciers that carved their way to the sea, leaving massive boulders in their wakes. And on most of those lakes, I'd hazard a guess, those rocks end up taking on a life of their own. Ours certainly has. Leaping off it is a rite of passage for some, a yearly ritual for others, and a daily way to kill time for those who spend their entire summers on the pristine little Hancock County lake.

Part of the reason for our attraction to it, I suppose, is that it has a cool name.

Lucerne has its Elephant Rock. Sebago has Frye's Leap. And Beech Hill has (I'm not making this up) Junk of Pork.

Actually, according to the 1981 U.S. Department of Interior Geological Survey Map, it's called "Junk of Pork Rock."

Early speculation, which may have simply been a way for my father to get us to stop asking a question for which nobody had an answer, was that in order to understand the name, you had to think figuratively.

The pond, you see, wasn't always a pond. It was once a plateful of baked beans. And the rock? Well, it was bigger than a bean, so it had to be the pork.

Boats flock to "Junk of Pork" rock in Beech Hill Pond, while swimmers wait their turns to jump off. Photo by John Holyoke.

Some locals call it Chunk of Pork. Others (probably those too embarrassed to believe that its name is so absurd) simply call it "the rock."

And those who can remember thirty or forty summers on Beech Hill Pond (a club, thankfully, to which I belong) have shortened that awkward name, turning it into a one-word wonder. To us, it's just Junkapork.

Nobody seems to know how big Junkapork really is, nor how deep the water surrounding it may be. Some claim they've hit bottom when they jumped off. Others say that's impossible.

From the water, the rock looks like it's about the height of a three-meter diving board. Ten feet, give or take. From the top of Junkapork, it's entirely different.

Ten feet looks more like fifteen, or even twenty, if you're seven years old and have never taken the leap before—or even if you're forty-one and are left wondering when you'll outgrow the need to leap off rocks into cool, deep water.

On a recent sunny weekend, the water around Junkapork resembled a marina, with kayakers vying for space with party barges and speedboats. One after another, potential jumpers climbed the ladder, refurbished in recent years by an unknown Beech Hill camper, and joined those waiting their turn.

On this day, a group of teenage girls (complete with the requisite cell phones, safely ensconced in Zip-lock baggies), lounged for hours on top of the rock, calling friends and taking occasional cooling plunges.

Some jumpers were young. Some were older. Some had never jumped before. And others were wily veterans even at the age of eleven, like my niece, Alyssa.

Alyssa's thirteen-year-old brother, Ryan, enjoys an occasional leap off Junkapork.

Alyssa? She lives for it.

"Junkapork, Junkapork, Junkapork," she'll whisper in my ear, a few dozen times a day until I finally agree to fire up the boat and take her there.

Once there, she's nothing but a no-nonsense Junkapork jumper. No twists. No tricks. Just jump after jump after jump, trying to get in as many leaps as possible before her mother and I pull the plug and head back to shore.

"She said she'd jump all day, or until she got hungry, if you let her," my sister Lori told me the other day.

Over the years, Junkapork has become many things for many visitors. For some, it's a mild way to address a fear of heights or water. For others, it becomes the way to prove, finally, that they're "big enough" to do what their siblings have done for years. And for still others, Junkapork seems to supply exactly what's needed whether you know what you need or not.

The special places we visit often have that effect, I figure.

A few years ago, a friend who was finally coming to terms with an especially depressing divorce visited camp and joined other friends for a trip to Junkapork. While diving off the boat to prepare for his first-ever leap, he resurfaced with what I assumed was bad news.

"My watch fell off," he said.

It was growing dark, and we couldn't find the timepiece anywhere. After a few leaps off the rock, he returned to the boat. I promised to search for his watch later.

"Don't worry about it," he said with a weary grin. "My ex gave it to me. I think I lost it for a reason."

Perhaps so. Perhaps not.

But thinking back on that night spent among friends, with one man's troubles seemingly washed away by that cool Beech Hill water, his words make more sense.

All because of Junkapork.

8. Give 'em a Wave

We Mainers are sometimes told (by those unfortunate folks we love to describe as being "From Away") that things are different here. Most of the time, our visitors mean that in a good way (or, at least, we Mainers convince ourselves that they do).

But sometimes, they don't mean it in a good way at all. Sometimes, our slow-paced life is irksome. So is finding out it has historically been hard to find a cup of Starbucks coffee in these parts and that in some towns, the sidewalks do, in fact, roll up at 9 p.m. (or earlier on weekdays).

Drive down a dirt road, which real Mainers likely call a camp road, and you'll find out exactly how different Mainers can be. Hop into any boat with any Mainer on any lake in the state, and you'll learn the same thing.

We're not unfriendly (as you may have been led to believe). We're not obstinate (for the most part). In fact, it seems an unwritten Maine rule that when you drive on a camp road or pilot a boat, you're required to be nearly, almost, pretty much downright hospitable.

Doubt it?

Look at a map. Find a lake. Turn off on a camp road that will get you there, and prepare to be amazed.

Camp road drivers don't honk their horns. Ever. Unless, that is, a stubborn moose refuses to yield his ground and let you pass even ten minutes or so after announcing your presence to the furry-but-somewhat-dimwitted behemoth. At that point, honking is also permitted by unwritten state rule.

And (here's the important part) camp-road drivers and boaters almost always wave.

"Who was that?" I am often asked, while ferrying unsuspecting non-Mainers to a lake or camp.

"Don't know," I tell them.

"So why did you wave?"

Good question. And while my answer might not satisfy non-Mainers led to believe that Pine Tree Staters are a bit . . . well . . . set in our ways, it is an answer nonetheless: Because that's the way it's always been. If you waved at every car you encountered in Bangor or Brewer or Presque Isle or Fort Kent, it wouldn't be practicable, of course. But in the woods? Or on the water? It just seems like the thing to do. And most times, Mainers don't even realize that we've done it. A few years back, a friend clued me in to the whole "wave-on-a-camp-road" phenomenon (just after I'd waved at an unfamiliar vehicle, no doubt) and told me how different we Mainers really are. He had recently returned from a mandatory out-of-state stint and was happy to be back.

"I love it that people here wave back," he told me.

To him, that wave wasn't the simple gesture it has become to so many of us.

To him, it meant he was home.

And to many of us, it still means the same thing . . . whether we take the time to realize it or not.

Memorable Mainers

Many stories in this book are designed to entertain or make you chuckle. Others are meant to be read in a different way. This chapter includes columns about people I was fortunate to cross paths with over the years.

All these people sat with me and trusted me with their stories, knowing that I'd share those tales with thousands of strangers. There are few greater honors, I figure, than to be allowed to tell someone else's story. Not wanting to offer a one-off tale about someone and leave you wondering about the following years, I've included the thoughts I shared with *Bangor Daily News* readers after their deaths.

9. Struck By Lightning

Charles Kimball has been heading deep into the Maine woods to Caucomgomoc Lake since 1924. Or maybe it was 1925. He doesn't remember exactly. He has spent plenty of time in the northwest corner of Piscataquis County, catching trout, hunting deer and birds, and enjoying time with family and friends.

On October 1, Kimball nearly died there.

That he didn't, and that he tells the tale of near death with a grin on his face, says something about the eighty-five-year-old former dentist from Carmel. So, too, do the words he shared with his son, Curt, when Curt visited him in the hospital.

Curt, you see, knew what his father had been through. He'd seen what one random bolt of lightning had done to the clothing his dad was wearing on his first day of a bird-hunting trip. And he told his dad how lucky he'd been to survive.

"I'm a tough son of a bitch, aren't I?" Charles Kimball asked his son.

The answer, of course, is yes.

The first of October began as many others have for Kimball. He rose early and had breakfast with his son, Charlie. They talked about plans for that day's hunt. Then he adjourned to the outhouse before heading out.

He didn't come back.

"Way off, four or five miles, I had heard a rumble of thunder," Charles Kimball said on Friday, telling his tale from a hospital bed at Eastern Maine Medical Center.

But he never had any idea that a storm was really brewing or that lightning was imminent.

"I never, ever thought anything about it," he said. "This was just like a shot of lightning out of a clear, blue sky. I couldn't believe it. Even now, I can't. But I know I have to."

All he knows is that he woke up some time later and found out that he was in trouble.

"It knocked me right over sideways and out cold," he said. "When I regained consciousness, I started to straighten up and reach out, and I couldn't feel my hands or my arms. I said, 'Oh my God. I've had a stroke.'"

A few minutes later, Charlie headed outside and found his father. Charles said his son has since told him that the scene was terrifying.

"Things were pretty horrible," Charles Kimball said. "[Charlie] said he's read all of [Stephen] King's novels, but he's never seen anything as horrible as I was. I was in shreds and tatters and everything else."

Charlie quickly packed his father into the car and headed for Millinocket, typically an hour and a half drive. It didn't take nearly that long, Charles said.

"Frankly, I didn't know if I was gonna get to Millinocket or not," Charles said. "I have never hurt so in my life. It hurt awful."

The remnants of his clothing paint a vivid picture of the ordeal—the lightning blew a two-inch-wide hole in his hunting hat and made an even bigger gash in his shirt. His left pant-leg looked like it lost a battle with a lawnmower, and the exiting voltage caused his left shoe to explode along the stitching. His socks—and nearly everything else he was wearing—were scorched black.

Now, as he recovers during a second stint at EMMC, the burns on his body are beginning to heal. Still, they're nasty reminders of the ordeal, as is his shattered right eardrum. Charles Kimball knows he's lucky. But that fact doesn't come as a complete surprise to him, either.

Eight years ago, he went to a Florida hospital with chest pains that turned out to be a mild heart attack. Two or three days later, as he recuperated, he had another. And it wasn't mild at all.

"They had to put the paddles to me three different times to get me back," he said. "It was so bad, they couldn't operate. Nobody thought I was ever gonna be back."

He was, and he credits the therapy he later received at EMMC.

"They made a man out of me," he said.

Two years later, an aneurysm threatened his life again. Two days after an operation—and just hours after a doctor decided to keep him for another day, just to be safe—he ended up on the operating table again.

"I lost two quarts of blood before they even got me on the table," he said. "If I'd been anywhere else in the world, that would have been it. I've been lucky. They say a cat's got nine lives. I guess I've got three or four more left."

Charles Kimball is old enough to remember the good old days at Caucomgomoc.

"When we first started going up there, if we'd go up for four or five days and if we didn't catch a brook trout that weighed over four or five pounds, we thought something was wrong," he said. "If you get one now that weighs two pounds, two pounds and a half, you think you have a monster."

Kimball remembers his first fishing trip, when his father tied three separate flies onto the leader and told him to drift them down a swiftly flowing stream. That was back in the 1920s. Kimball was seven or eight. And he'll never forget hooking onto three fish at once, nor the fact that his dad refused to let him relinquish the rod.

"He coached me and coached me and coached me," he said. Finally, Charles landed all three fish. The trout weighed in at a collective 14 pounds, 2 ounces.

His father also coached him several years later, after taking Charles to a tryout with the Boston Red Sox. The Sox wanted to assign him to the club's Single A team in Little Rock, Arkansas, Charles recalls. On the ride home, his father asked a simple question.

"Do you still want to be a dentist?"

When Charles answered in the affirmative, his father laid down the law.

"He said, 'You've answered my question. You're not playing ball anymore. That's it.' Well, we had a fight and I didn't speak to him for two or three weeks. But you know what they said: The man that controls the purse strings controls the boy."

After attending the University of Maine and Harvard, Charles Kimball became a dentist. He served with the Air Force in World War II, after finding a considerate medical colleague who overlooked that he'd been turned down by the Navy because of an old football injury . . . and color blindness . . . and flat feet.

The spunky Kimball quickly found out that military life didn't suit him too well, as he took some grief from a flight surgeon.

"He says, 'How in the name of God did you ever get in here?'" Charles Kimball recalled. "I said, 'That's not the question: How in the name of God do I get out?' From that time on, I never had any trouble with him."

Charles Kimball is also young enough to relish the times he spends at Caucomgomoc today . . . and tomorrow. That's right: He's already planning to head back.

"I told the doctor, 'You've got from now until the first of November, because I'm going deer hunting on the first of November," Kimball said.

"I can't travel the way I used to, but still and all, I can be out there, and I can walk a ways, and do this and do that. And I can do some bird hunting, too. That's easy enough."

The doctor's reply? "He said he'd do the best that he could," Kimball said with a chuckle.

One way or another, Kimball figures he'll be out there in the woods when deer season opens.

"I'm going up there the first," he said. "I don't give a damn. There's no sense laying back and feeling sorry for yourself."

10. Afterword: Charles Kimball

Columns come and columns go. Three times a week for the past seven years (give or take a few days off here and there), I've written an outdoors column for the *Bangor Daily News*. Some column topics are quickly forgotten. Others, fortunately, are much different. I remember them— and the people who inspired them—like I'd written them yesterday. Seven years ago—October 12, 2002, to be exact—I wrote one such piece. It was my fourth as an outdoor columnist, and contained an amazing tale that I still recount several times a year.

In a chance meeting at a Bangor bookstore, an acquaintance told me that his dad had been struck by lightning . . . while bird-hunting. . . while in the outhouse. You don't have to be much of a journalist to recognize that scenario as serious column fodder, especially if you're a columnist new to the outdoor-writing game. I quickly arranged a meeting with the victim, who was recuperating in a Bangor hospital.

The interview was one of the most enjoyable I've ever had. The eighty-five-year-old subject was kind and engaging and eager to talk. We spent quite a bit of time together, me listening, him telling several tales (including, eventually, the one I'd come to hear).

The lightning had burned a hole in his hunting hat. One hunting boot was blown apart. And in his hospital bed, nursing serious injuries, Charles Kimball was able to chuckle at his own expense. I never forgot that.

The particulars of the incident were remarkable. Kimball survived the lightning bolt, suffered a shattered eardrum, and considered himself lucky. Eight years earlier, he'd suffered two heart attacks over a three-day span and nearly died on an operating table.

"They had to put the paddles to me three different times to get me back," Kimball told me that day. "It was so bad, they couldn't operate. Nobody thought I was ever gonna be back."

Two years after that, an aneurysm threatened his life, and he ended up in the hospital again. Again, he bounced back.

At the hospital on that October afternoon in 2002, Kimball told me he didn't want his story to come across inappropriately, and he hoped that I'd leave out the worst of the outhouse parts. I lobbied for their inclusion, telling him that they would make the column a great read. Before I left his bedside that day, he relented, slightly.

"Do what you want," he told me, grasping my hand in farewell. "I trust you. I'm sure you'll do the right thing."

I'm not sure how why he made that assumption after spending part of afternoon with a total stranger, but as I left, I suspected his faith had been misplaced. I debated for hours, wrote the column three different ways, and ultimately proved him right.

I left out the juicy parts.

On Friday, seven years after the lightning strike that nearly took his life, Charles Kimball died in a Bangor health care facility. He was ninety-two. I saw the obituary in Monday's paper and fondly recalled our short time together.

Kimball was a dentist by trade and a World War II veteran by choice. He completed a four-year program at the University of Maine in two years. He was also an outdoorsman his entire life.

Kimball was married to his wife, Ruth, for fifty-three years before her death in 1995. They had four children, ten grandchildren, and thirteen great-grandchildren.

His obituary points out that he "loved nothing more than to sit in the screened in porch of his hunting and fishing camp at Caucomgomoc Lake in the evenings after his day's activities in the north Maine woods."

During our visit seven years ago, Charles Kimball told me that one of his proudest sporting moments came when he was seven or eight years old. His own father had tied three flies to a leader and told him to drift the rig through a particular spot on a stream. Kimball did, and hooked three fish at once. His father refused to take the rod, figuring Charles would figure things out on his own.

"He coached me and coached me and coached me," Charles Kimball told me that day.

And after a lengthy fight, the coaching paid off: Charles caught all three fish. They weighed a total of 14 pounds, 2 ounces.

I never spoke to Charles Kimball again after our interview in his hospital room. That's the way this business often works. Columnists move on to other columns. Column subjects continue living their lives. But his tale—and his gracious manner on that memorable day—still resonate. His family, I'm sure, is hurting right now. Nothing I write will change that.

But in infrequent conversations with Curt and Denise Kimball, and their daughters, Denise Jr. and Michelle, I learned how special their father, father-in-law, and grandfather was to them and how lucky they felt to have been able to spend so much time with him.

Charles Kimball lived ninety-two years. He made an impact on the people he knew and those he loved. His family members probably won't be surprised to learn he even taught important lessons to those that he'd just met.

I trust you. I'm sure you'll do the right thing.

11. The Jim Carter Show

Early each spring, Jim Carter recalls, his father often made pilgrimages to the camp he loved on Munsungan Stream.

"As soon as it would warm up a bit, and the snow was gone, he'd say, 'I'm going to go in and watch the green climb Norway.'"

For those who've never visited Jim Carter at Munsungan Hunting and Fishing Club—he opened his father's old cabin as a sporting camp back in 1998—that phrase likely sounds puzzling. To those who have fallen under Munsungan's spell—men like Jimmy Spellman of Masardis—the phrase "watching the green climb Norway" makes perfect sense.

Sit for a spell in front of the main camp, the one that sits just above one of the most beautiful stream pools you'll ever find, and it will make sense to you, too.

"Munsungan is a state of mind," says Spellman, a frequent visitor. "It really is. It's a magical place."

So sit down for a bit. Look off to the right and enjoy. See that mountain, the lush, colorful one standing sentinel over Little Munsungan? That's Norway Bluff. And the green climbing Norway? That was just Ray Carter's way of saying he wanted to be here, in camp, when the area finally shook off the insults of another harsh winter and the foliage began to slowly creep up that pretty little bluff.

Ray Carter died here, his son tells you, speaking as softly as he ever will. Jim Carter says that when his time is up, his ashes will be scattered here, too.

"I get choked up just talking about it," he says. "[Dad] told his cousin about two weeks before he died, 'If I'm lucky I'll die at camp with Jim.'"

Ray Carter would have been eighty-seven that fall. Jim Carter found his dad sitting in a favorite rocking chair, his hand resting on his English setter's head. Ray Carter had been dead for four or five hours, his son recounts. And his loyal dog never moved.

Carter's Munsungan Hunting and Fishing Club is about forty miles via Ashland, ninety miles if you drive from Medway, and about a million miles from the worries and problems of your own home or office.

The woods are thick, the pace is slow, and the host is, well, "crusty" probably works as well as any other adjective you'll find. And each year, more and more people are deciding to head into the Maine woods and spend a few days enjoying, as one sporting supplier recently called it, "The Jim Carter Show."

"It's the location. It isn't me," Carter says. "I cook late, bitch at my guests. It's the location and the aesthetics of the camp [that draws them], and they have to put up with me to get it. That's what I tell 'em."

Carter is comfortable in a crowd or by himself in the middle of the woods. He loves to hunt and fish but would just as soon lean back in a chair, re-light his pipe for the twentieth time and recite his favorite Robert Service poetry. Sit around his wood stove, and you're as apt to end up debating politics or learning the history of the Maine woods as you are telling fishing stories or debating the merits of various streamer flies.

"You are a neophyte," he booms, only half in jest, when mention of one of his favorite outdoor authors elicits raised eyebrows. "I can see I've got to put together a reading list for you."

Ray Carter and some friends had the camp built back in 1938, and Jim learned to love the place early on. Jim grew up in Washburn, got into farming, and when his seed potato business began to struggle in the 1990s, he changed course and headed into the woods.

Jim Carter, courtesy of Hannah Carter.

"I walked out [of the potato business] with my shirt and a little bit [of money]," he says. "Both kids were out of college, and my biggest responsibility was feeding two dogs."

There was no road into the club at that point. Carter built one. By 1998, his permit allowed him to take in ten commercial guests at a time. To Carter, turning the place into a sporting camp seemed a perfect idea.

"I can say that people have been hunting and fishing here for 10,000 years, because we've dug [artifacts that prove it]," Carter says.

Guests began to show up. They fished Munsungan Lake and Little Munsungan and fell in love with the stream itself. They kept coming back. Today there are two camps for guests and one main lodge that Carter stays in. And business has never been better.

"Now I'm taking in more money in some weeks than I took in that first year," Carter says. "And sixty-eight percent of my guests [this year], from the start until the first of July, are repeats or are coming with repeats."

That was the case earlier this week, as Spellman, a "repeat," brought some other friends in. Bruce Gullifer of Scarborough had been here before, but Eric Day of Bangor hadn't. Jamie Higgins of Bangor filled out the fishing party. Day says that he had fished Munsungan before; and had been hearing stories about Carter for years. And that's why he was in camp.

"That's part of the whole thing for me," Day says. "His stories, the tradition, more than catching fish."

But make no mistake about one thing: The good-natured Carter runs a (somewhat) tight ship (sometimes). And if you travel to Munsungan Hunting and Fishing Club, you're entering his domain.

His stories will stretch on and lead seamlessly into the next (but he'll listen just as curiously when you tell yours). The meals may come a bit later than you expect. And if you sit at his dinner table with your hat on, well, let's just say you won't be wearing it for long.

Carter bakes pies or cookies each day ("Cakes will sit there and go moldy, but everyone loves pie," he says), and sometimes guides as well.

Despite juggling countless tasks—there are no other employees here and Carter is literally the chef, head guide, and chief bottle washer— everything eventually works out just fine. And the more flexible the guests, the more fun they'll have. Case-in-point: Carter believes that fishing is a lot of fun. But he also believes that there's much more to life than that.

Munsungan has fish. But it has much, much more if you're willing to notice. Some evenings, when the fishing's slow or the guests are adventurous, Carter asks them if they really, truly want to continue trolling or if they're up for other options. Often, they agree with their guide that it might be time to pull in the lines and do something different.

"I call it 'chasing the sunset,'" Carter says, a smile beginning to form. "We start in the stream and head up the lake, and we just chase that sunset to the other end of Munsungan."

Deep in the Maine woods, after all the green has climbed Norway, and after plenty of fish have been caught, that's not a bad way to spend the final minutes of daylight.

Many of his guests realize that.

"When you sit in a canoe and observe Norway Bluff and the mountains, it's almost difficult to explain to someone unless they've seen it," Spellman says. "It's just that special."

12. Afterword: Jim Carter

Seven years ago this June, I spent an uncomfortably wonderful weekend deep in the Maine woods, learning about the history and mystique of the Munsungan Hunting and Fishing Club. My host, both the source of my discomfort and primary reason the trip was memorable, was Jim Carter, the camp's owner and its sole guide. Carter was, to be perfectly clear, opinionated. He was just as apt to spend a half hour expounding on national politics as he was the fishing on Munsungan Lake. If you disagreed with him, he'd tell you that you were wrong. Then he'd tell you why. Then he'd tell you again. Carter was prone to reciting Robert Service poems, from memory, even if his visitors had no interest in poetry or had not even heard of Robert Service.

On my way into the woods that weekend, I stopped by an outfitter's store, and he asked where I was heading. When I told him, he laughed.

"You're going to see the Jim Carter Show," he told me. I chuckled along, politely, not knowing what he was talking about. That weekend I learned.

And last week, I was saddened to learn that the Jim Carter Show has signed off. Carter, after a battle with cancer, died on December 28. He was seventy. Munsungan will never be the same.

Jim Carter loved his peaceful camp on Little Munsungan, some forty miles from Ashland, or, if you choose, about ninety miles via Medway. Jim Carter was understandably proud that his father, Ray, along with some friends, built the camp in 1938. Ray Carter, an Army veteran and potato farmer, spent a lot of time at Munsungan. He fished. He hunted. And eventually, he died right there, within sight of the prettiest little fishing holes you're ever going to find in the Maine woods.

"[Dad] told his cousin, about two weeks before he died, 'If I'm lucky, I'll die here at camp with Jim,'" Carter told me that weekend, choking out the words.

Ray Carter did, indeed, die at camp, at the age of eighty-six. Jim Carter wasn't there but found his dad, several hours later, sitting in a favorite rocking chair, his hand resting on his English setter's head. During our visit, Jim Carter solemnly told his guests that when his time came, he wanted his ashes scattered at Munsungan as well.

Jim himself built the road that leads to Munsungan Hunting and Fishing Club, and in 1998 he began welcoming paying guests to his new sporting camp. Once at the camp, sports quickly learned they were not only deep in the Maine woods, they were also in an entirely different time zone than the one they'd left. Let's call it Carter Standard Time, if you please.

While Carter was a gracious host and loved being around people, even the most well-heeled guests learned that at Munsungan, there was no use cajoling the pipe-smoking head guide. Dinner would be good. Great, sometimes. The pies would be fresh, baked that day. You'd eventually sit down to eat. After a drink or two. After a story or two or four.

"I cook late, bitch at my guests," Carter told me that weekend, after we'd sat down to dinner at about 9 p.m. "It's the location and the aesthetics of camp [that draws them], and they have to put up with me to get it."

He did cook late. He did bitch at guests. And that weekend, I learned that I was, in Carter's words, "a neophyte." For the record, he called me more than that. Seeing as how this is a family publication, I'm leaving out the choice adjective that he used quite frequently.

"I can see I've got to put together a reading list for you," he told me, only half in jest.

For the past seven years, I've half-expected to receive that reading list. And over the past seven years, I've learned that Jim Carter was correct—I was a neophyte when it came to the big north woods, and the lands and waters that he loved. He had been there. Done that. And he damn-well knew it.

A few years later, I showed him that I'd learned at least one of my lessons, when we reconnected at the Eastern Maine Sportsman's Show in Orono.

During my time in camp, I remembered, Carter had talked at length about my predecessors on the outdoor beat at the *Bangor Daily News*. He told stories about Tom Hennessey. He shared tales about Bud Leavitt. And he talked for a long while about Bill Geaghan, who toiled at this paper before I was born. I sat and listened, and absorbed as much as I could.

Much later, at the sportsman's show, I walked up to Carter's booth and handed him an audio book of "Nature I Loved," which *Bangor Daily News* staffers had unearthed in a closet, and which we were giving away during the show. Its author was Bill Geaghan.

For once, Carter had little to say. He just smiled, wiped away what I thought was a tear, and shook my hand.

"Thank you," he said softly. "I really like this book."

"I know you do," I told him. "I was listening the night when I learned that I was a neophyte."

Carter laughed at that, and each time I saw him, he told me I'd have to return to his special place in the Maine woods. It was a place where he loved "to watch the green climb Norway," his way of describing the gradual reawakening that took place each spring on nearby Norway Bluff. It was a place he liked to "chase the sunset," with adventurous guests who weren't in a hurry to get back to camp at the end of a long day.

"We start in the stream and head up the lake, and we just chase that sunset to the other end of Munsungan," he told me.

We didn't chase the sunset that day. Some day, perhaps I'll return, and try it on my own. Without Jim Carter aboard, I'm sure the experience won't be nearly as uncomfortable.

I'm also sure it won't be nearly as good.

13. A Legend Named "Wiggie"

As the skies opened up and a torrential downpour turned the roof of Wiggie Robinson's pickup truck into a rolling steel drum, the veteran Maine guide glanced at his son and I and began to shake his head.

"We might just be taking a ride tonight," he said, pointing the truck toward a fishy location an hour northwest of his camp.

Sitting under black skies, it seemed likely that the massive thunderstorm I'd driven through most of the way from Bangor to the West Branch of the Penobscot would, indeed, wash out our scheduled evening of fishing. Jay Robinson and I each smiled and handed Wiggie our unanimous verdict: "Doesn't matter to us. A drive sounds fine."

Ideally, of course, our journey up the Golden Road would end in success. The skies would clear. The hatch of juicy green drakes would be huge, and hungry trout would feast on them as well as our proffered imitations. But if it didn't turn out that way? None of us really cared all that much. The evening already had been a success, I figured.

Jay and I had already had a bit of fun when we discovered at a logjam of cars stopped on the road to his father's camp.

"You got a moose?" Jay Robinson asked the throng of sight-seers.

They did, and we spied a big bull with a massive rack fifty yards away, knee-deep in the West Branch. The moose dipped his head in the water, looking for forage, as the crowd cooed to him and tried to get his attention.

"Can you call him when it's not in the rut?" I asked Jay, a guide and successful moose hunter.

Sheepishly, Jay grunted to the moose, and after repeated coaxing from the crowd, I tried my own off-key call. The moose may have paid attention, or he may not have.

It didn't really matter to the assembled tourists, many of whom spoke in a cadence that gave away their southern roots. Just seeing a couple of Mainers trying to speak to one of their own made them laugh, and they thanked us for our efforts before we drove off.

That, though, was earlier in the day, before the rain began to fall again, and before the evening's trip seemed in jeopardy. On the way to one of Wiggie Robinson's many "secret" fishing destinations, and on the way back, to be honest, the stories flowed. Place names roll off the tongues of both guides, and every hillock, stream, and gully have an appropriate label.

Earlier, Jay explained that a mucky little clearing alongside the Golden Road was called "The Salad Bar," since moose were often seen browsing there at sunset.

Wiggie, eighty-three years old now but still eager and able to hike to all of his favorite remote ponds, recalled his early days in the region he calls "Katahdin Country." When he was ten, he and his eight-year-old brother caught a ride into Baxter State Park and stayed with a warden all summer.

"We thought we were the real Maine Guides," he said. "And I guess we were. We knew every trail in the park, and we'd show people where they were. We'd climb Katahdin every day. Sometimes twice a day."

Maine guide Wiggie Robinson. Photo by John Holyoke.

The following year, the Robinson boys didn't hitch a ride to Baxter, Robinson said. They just packed up their bedrolls, some beans, and walked into the woods. He was eleven.

On this day, as the road unfurled, rain continued to pelt us. Sometimes, it relented, but most of the time, it did nothing of the sort.

"It'll keep the dust down, anyway," Wiggie told us as we crept through another downpour.

Eventually, we arrived at the appropriate North Maine Woods gate to the sound of even more thunder. But then our wishes were granted—nearly.

As we drove the last dozen or so miles to our destination, the sky to the northwest was blue. The sun shone through. The road turned dusty and dry once again. We fished late into the evening that night, and I'd like to be able to tell you that everything turned out perfectly.

The green drakes did hatch, after all. The sunset was beautiful. But as we returned to the truck after fruitlessly flogging the water, Wiggie Robinson's words again rang true.

"We might just be taking a ride tonight," he had said.

That, we had. Rest assured, none of us would have rather stayed home, either.

14. Afterword: Wiggie Robinson

Wilmot "Wiggie" Robinson didn't answer to "Mister," least of all from people he considered his friends. That's something I'll always remember. I tried to call him Mr. Robinson once. It only seemed proper; I was, after all, forty-three years younger than the renowned Maine guide from Millinocket and was just trying to show him the proper level of respect—just like my mother had always taught me. Wiggie didn't cotton much to that notion.

"Wiggie," he corrected me, and although I can't remember all the subsequent details, I'm certain that he was grinning broadly. "I'm Wiggie."

To all of his friends, that's exactly who he was—Wiggie. And as I learned over the ensuing years, it was extremely difficult to meet the man without ending up being his friend. Nearly two weeks ago, Wiggie Robinson died in his vegetable garden. He was eighty-five and had just delivered a birthday present to his wife of sixty-one years, Joyce. It was a bouquet of home-grown flowers, no doubt lovingly arranged, and delivered (I'm sure) with a huge grin.

When I met Wiggie, he was the guide I'd been hearing about for years—the guy who, I later learned, caught a ride into Baxter State

Park at the age of ten, with his eight-year-old brother in tow, and unofficially began guiding tourists up Mount Katahdin.

I was new to the outdoor writing game, but Wiggie had been doing it for years. He had no reason to go out of his way to make me feel more comfortable in my new job. He had no reason to offer to show me some of his favorite spots or to take me (along with his son, Jay) on my first actual woodcock hunt. No reason, that is, save this: Being nice to people is what Wiggie was all about.

Wiggie was a small man, wiry and strong, with a spring in his step that belied his advancing years. I followed him and Jay over well-worn paths through Baxter State Park, and through prickly bird covers, and often struggled to keep up. Every time I saw him, his eyes would light up, and he would smile broadly. Then he'd say something nice to me.

Every time.

You undoubtedly read quite a bit about Wiggie Robinson last week, in the wake of his death. And although a long-awaited week of vacation relieved me of deadline responsibilities for a spell, it didn't relieve me of this responsibility to tell you a few things about the man.

About the man who loved his wife and family and God. About the man who always had something positive to say to everybody he'd pass. No, I didn't know Wiggie Robinson that long, nor that well. But I do know this: Every time we'd see each other, and every time we'd part company after sharing a few tales, he'd say the same thing. *It's good to see you, my friend.*

To be perfectly clear, Wiggie Robinson didn't have a shortage of friends. Not by a long shot. When he entered a room full of strangers, he was the kind of guy who'd leave knowing everybody by name and having made plans to catch up with many of them in the woods or on the waters he loved.

No, being a friend of Wiggie's didn't mean you were a member of a small, exclusive fraternity.

However, it did mean that you were extremely fortunate to have crossed paths with this one-of-a-kind gentleman.

That's what I'll remember.

It was good to see you, my friend.

15. "I Miss My Dad"

October has always been a special month for Jay Robinson. Put a blaze-orange hat on his head, a 20-gauge shotgun in his hands and an eager bird dog in front of him and life is nearly perfect. Even after the Millinocket paper mill went belly-up—his job vanishing along with it—the first full month of autumn was a time to be savored, appreciated, and cherished.

Opening day of bird season is a day to be celebrated, after all. Even when the birds are scarce and the weather is warm, you know that things will change. Eventually, the nights will grow chillier. The trees will quickly gain color and then, after a day of strong rain or wind, relinquish those leaves to the forest floor.

About that time, when the visibility gets better and the flights of woodcock start their annual migration south—stopping at regular haunts near Medway and Chester and Woodville—Robinson figures it's time to get serious about hunting.

This year, though, things will just feel different. Look in the back of his well-worn Chevy truck—300,000 miles and still chugging— and you'll understand part of the reason why. There, in one kennel, lies Sadie, an eight-year-old English pointer with a great nose for

Jay Robinson. Photo by John Holyoke.

birds. In the kennel next door lies Katie. She's ten and although she, too, is officially Jay's dog now, she unintentionally serves as a constant reminder of how much things can change between hunting trips.

A year ago, you see, Katie didn't belong to Jay Robinson. No, last year she was Wiggie Robinson's prized pooch.

"I miss my dad," Jay Robinson says softly, shortly after joining a couple of hunters for a day in some of his favorite bird covers.

Seasons change. Years pass. And regrettably, fathers do, too. That's just the way it works. And knowing that fact doesn't make it any easier. Not even when your dad dies at eighty-five after living a long, full life, as Jay Robinson's dad did back in June.

"I miss my dad," Jay Robinson says again, a bit later. "I think once the weather cools off, I'll get a little more enthused. I'm taking a guy next week that we've guided for over thirty years."

Then, of course, the memories will continue to flow. Birds shot and missed. Dogs that have come and gone. Hunts that were great and not so great. The Robinson men were both guides and spent hours together hiking into remote trout ponds, tracking deer, and watching their bird dogs point grouse and woodcock. Come October, the birds got top billing, and both men made a point to set time aside for their regular trips afield.

"If the weather wasn't bad [on opening day], we usually always went out," Jay Robinson says. "And the last week of the season, we were mostly done guiding and we saved that week for the two of us. That's when the flights [of migrating woodcock] were in good, the leaves are all gone, it's a bit cooler. We had more fun that last week than anything, really."

This week, Jay Robinson has been largely alone with his thoughts, as he travels from one bird-hunting spot to another. No matter where he goes, his father awaits. That, too, is the way it works.

"The first day I think I moved twenty birds, but I didn't shoot good that day," Jay Robinson says.

The next day, things got a bit better, but still not great.

"I haven't moved a lot of grouse. That doesn't mean I shouldn't have shot a few," he says. "I'm a little rusty. I think I miss the old man."

Together, the Robinsons made a great team. Wiggie Robinson knew everything there was to know about the woods, it seemed. Jay Robinson was the sponge who walked alongside as a child, soaking in all that knowledge. When Wiggie's advancing years—and likely his years of working in the cacophony of the same paper mill—cost him much of his hearing, Jay was there to help.

Year after year, Jay increasingly served as his father's ears in the field, telling Wiggie when a dog's collar bell had stopped ringing. Silent dogs are often pointing dogs, you see. And that's what the game's all about. On Thursday, Sadie and Katie worked hard in hot, miserable conditions. They pointed a few birds, and Jay and a visitor each shot one and missed others. Katie is still adjusting to her new master, it seems, and may well have memories of her own of the sinewy old man who followed her through the woods year after year.

Seasons change. Life changes. We all adapt, the best we can. Not that it's easy, mind you. Jay Robinson is grateful for the time he got to spend with his father and the valuable lessons he learned. Consciously or unconsciously, he passes those lessons along to others every time he guides a hunter.

Tracks. Scat. Trees. Mushrooms. Bird cover that looks promising. Dogs: present, past and future. All are likely to be discussed at length. And all were topics of conversation when he and his dad went into the woods.

Season after season. Year after year. Until …

Jay Robinson remembers the time, not too many months ago, when he, his son Michael, and Wiggie took the dogs into the woods to sniff out some birds. There would be other days to come, of course. Other, better days, when birds were plentiful, the leaves had dropped, and everyone was shooting well.

"Little did I know," Jay Robinson says, softly, shaking his head. "Little did I know."

16. Rescue!

Lisa Bates knows her recurring, nagging thought makes little sense. She's lucky to be alive, after all. She survived a helicopter crash. She dragged the injured pilot out of the wreckage, then hiked out of dense woods to find help. She is, some might say, a hero.

Still, she keeps thinking of the tree. Fixating on the tree. Wondering about the tree.

"I want to go back to the site, I know it sounds stupid, to figure out what tree [we hit]," the twenty-seven-year-old Belfast woman says, leaning forward in a chair at her aunt's camp on Pleasant Lake, where she's recovering from her injuries. "Because I remember seeing a tree, and I remember it looking like an ash tree. And I really want to know."

Bates was working as the assistant project coordinator on a Unity College bear study last Wednesday when the chopper she was riding in crashed. She and Ed Friedman—the two were working together for the first time—were trying to locate a signal from a bear fitted with a radio collar.

The duo took off from Waterville at four in the afternoon. After cruising toward Burnham and checking out some bald eagle nests, they received a faint signal from the bear's collar. Not long after that, they had tracked the bear to some dense woods. And not long after that, something went wrong. Bates remembers the chopper losing power.

"I just said, 'What's happening?'" she recalled. Friedman replied that he didn't know.'"

Then the chopper was spinning. The trees were getting closer.

"The first tree that we crashed through, the first limbs, I remember that," Bates said. "And I remember being really, really scared. And then, really, really sad. And something else. And then black."

Friedman is a fifty-eight-year-old volunteer pilot for LightHawk, a nonprofit group that provides gratis flying services for conservation organizations across the nation. The flight was the first undertaken as part of Unity College's bear research project, which was announced in

March. Field work began in May when Bates and others trapped black bears and fitted females with collars. The goal was to add data to Maine Department of Inland Fisheries and Wildlife's long-term bear research while providing training opportunities for Unity College students.

Bates explained that in some cases, finding a radio-collared bear from the ground can be very difficult. Taking advantage of the chance to track a bear from the air made sense, she said. And with flight costs surpassing one hundred dollars an hour, the free flight offer by LightHawk was an opportunity that couldn't be passed up.

After nearly catching up with the bear she was tracking, Bates said, the helicopter crashed through trees from a height of fifty to sixty feet. At one moment, the craft was spinning. Then falling. Then, everything went dark. Bates now thinks she was unconscious for about forty-five minutes. And when she woke up, nothing made sense.

"I recognized that I was in the woods, in some sort of a crash, and I was freaking out," Bates said. "I didn't remember being in a helicopter. I didn't remember setting foot inside a helicopter. I didn't remember who Ed was. I didn't remember what LightHawk was."

She also doesn't remember removing her four-point harness or climbing over the still-unconscious Friedman. When Bates saw her telemetry gear and her personal camera, everything came rushing back. She knew why she was in a helicopter. She remembered the ash tree. And the bear.

"I was like, 'Ed! We're alive! Holy crap!'" Bates said. "Once I recognized my surroundings and what happened, it was like pure happiness. I was like, 'I cannot believe.' Because the last thing I felt was this complete, indescribable, terrible sadness that I was going to die."

Armed with that "pure happiness," which Bates attributes to adrenaline, and shock, and relief, she got to work.

Bates said she doesn't remember assessing her injuries but says she must have done so. Her left leg was sore and bleeding from a dime-sized puncture wound and she had cuts and bruises elsewhere. Her jaw was sore, and five days after the crash, it's still bruised. But she could stand. She could walk. And she could haul the seriously injured Friedman from the wreckage.

"Right by his head, fuel was leaking," Bates explained. "I'm like, 'We've got to get you out of here.' He's like, 'Yeah.' And he tried to move and he couldn't. He's like, 'I'm pinned.'"

Bates says she doesn't remember unfastening Friedman's four-point harness, but said that at some point, she pulled on the pilot's belt and turned him over, so that he was lying flat on the ground. Then she reached under his arms and began dragging him away from the helicopter.

"It was real painful on him. His ribs, his hip, his leg, his eye," Bates said. "I'd be like, 'OK. 1-2-3,' and then we'd drag, and he'd try to push with his right foot."

Making slow progress, Bates said, she moved Friedman about fifteen or twenty feet away from the helicopter. She wanted to move him farther, but said the pilot was in so much pain, they stopped. Bates says she has since learned that Friedman suffered a fractured and dislocated hip and compound fractures in his ankle, and said the pilot was quite sure he had broken ribs as well.

After helping make the pilot as comfortable as possible, Bates looked at her GPS unit, which was still on. She told Friedman what she'd decided to do.

"I just said, 'The [bear trap site] is six-tenths of a mile northeast. The road runs north-south. And so if I just go east it's the shortest distance and I'll just flag somebody down. The sun's setting. It's six o'clock. So

I'll just put the sun at my back and head east,'" Bates said. "I said, 'Are you OK with this plan?' And he said, 'It's the only one we have.'"

Bates equipped Friedman with some survival gear, including a granola bar, and took other gear with her. Unfortunately, their cell phones and the helicopter's radio were inoperable. She started bushwhacking, working her way through the woods toward a road. For about two hundred yards, she used orange flagging tape to carefully mark her route. Then she heard a car that she thought was nearby, and abandoned her flagging effort.

On Monday, she laughed when recounting that turn of events.

"One of [my] crewmates on the bear den crew gives me crap because I don't flag heavy and rely on my photographic memory to get me back to places," she said.

As it turns out, she wasn't as close to the road as she thought. But she kept walking east and got to it in good time. A passing motorist stopped and offered use of her phone. Bates' first called Friedman's wife and then 911 and then her boyfriend. By that time, others began arriving on the scene.

"Other people started to show up because there's a girl in the road with blood running down her leg," she said.

Bates initially wanted to stay on the scene. She handed her GPS unit to a volunteer firefighter who admitted he didn't know how to use it. Bates told him to find someone who did. But eventually, she was forced to leave the scene, with assistance.

"I refused the ambulance at first, until the sheriff gave me a strict talking-to: 'You were just in a helicopter crash. You need to go to the hospital,'" she said. "I was like, 'Yeah. I was just in a helicopter crash.'"

Both Bates and Friedman were taken to a Portland hospital. Friedman is still recovering there. Bates was released later that evening and was back home by 2 a.m. Thursday, according to her mother. Not long after that, she was headed back into the woods, to a family camp, to more fully recover.

Lisa Bates is not a wilderness first responder. She's a bear researcher. On Monday, while relaxing with family members, Bates attributed the experience she has gained over the past five years working on the DIF&W's bear study group to her reaction after the crash.

"Randy Cross training," she said when asked if she'd had any proper medical or emergency training. Cross is the longtime leader of the DIF&W's bear research group. He's the one who helped convince Bates that it makes perfect sense to crawl head-first into a bear's den in the middle of winter, all in the name of science. And his messages paid dividends last week.

"I really, honestly don't think I would have reacted in the way that I did had I not been in the line of work [that I am]," Bates said. "I've never come across anything like this in my life, but working for Randy on the bear crew, there are a lot of situations on a smaller scale [when] you put yourself into where you have to overcome irrational fear and your body's intense desire to run."

Bates' experience with the DIF&W bear study led to her being hired to help coordinate the Unity College project, according to the college project's coordinator, George Matula Jr.

Bates said when the DIF&W bear crew unwinds at the end of the day, "storytime" is a bit of a tradition. And Cross, the wildlife biologist, is chief storyteller.

"We talk about these certain [potentially frightening] circumstances a lot," Bates said. "Today when I talked to [Cross], I said, 'I think all the training finally came to a head, where it finally mattered.'"

But hero? Bates isn't ready to make that leap. That's a label for others.

"There was no other choice," she said. "That stuff had to be done. Ed had to be out of that helicopter. And we had to get out of the woods."

17. Return of the Native

Lindsay grew up here, on the edge of some of the state's deepest, least-developed woods, running from cabin to cabin of the traditional sporting camp that her parents owned, playing with the children of guests and sharing her living room with hunters, snowmobilers, and anglers. Not that she ever thought she'd want to own Mt. Chase Lodge herself, mind you.

"It was awesome and I hated it—all at the same time," she said, shaking her head at the memory and laughing. "I loved guests. I loved hanging out with them. Probably I was the most annoying kid ever, because if we ever had families staying and if they had kids that were my age, I would sleep in the cabins and we would have this great sleepover."

When she was about ten, she remembers earning twenty dollars per night in tips from hunters who'd send her running to fetch them bottles of beer they'd left on their cabin porches. Then, she began to grow up.

"I loved it until I became a teenager, and then I hated it," she said. "Because as a teenager, all I wanted was my own space. Somebody's always in my house. [I was] always having to have that face on."

And when she graduated from high school, she vowed she'd never return to run the lodge on the shore of Upper Shin Pond. Between then and now, a lot happened. Lindsay met Mike Downing. The couple hiked a long trail together and they fell in love. They worked in the hospitality business deep in the woods of Maine and Alaska. And eventually they decided that buying that lodge seemed like a pretty fine idea.

In 2016, Lindsay and her husband Mike Downing bought the place from her parents, Rick and Sara Hill. Consisting of five private cabins and eight bedrooms in the main building, the lodge first opened in 1960.

The new owners would likely tell you the purchase was just the latest great adventure they've shared. Together, they've reshaped Mt. Chase Lodge, changing focus from filling the bellies of hungry hunters to offering more sophisticated and scrumptious dinners by reservation, which locals drive miles to enjoy.

Their job responsibilities are strictly defined. Lindsay, energetic and outgoing, now eagerly puts on "that face" and concentrates on the customers. Mike, quiet and low-key, is skilled in the kitchen and provides the vision that fuels the lodge's commitment to food. Adding to their optimism and serving as one of the catalysts of their decision to pursue their dreams here is the presence of the year-old Katahdin Woods and Waters National Monument not far from their front door.

"We always knew we [were sitting on a] gold mine [if the national monument designation took place," Lindsay said. "It is the future for us."

When Mike graduated from Bates College with a degree in physics, he took a job in the insurance field and spent four and one-half years in an office cubicle he came to dread.

"I couldn't take it anymore, being stuck inside all day," he said. "That's when I decided to leave, and I was looking for some kind of trail job or national park job. I had one connection that got me into Maine Huts and Trails."

Mike had long loved to cook—his mom used to pay him to make her breakfast—and he got to work learning more about the field.

Meanwhile, Lindsay was living her own dream, teaching at an outdoor education center in California and looking to come back to her home state. While on a rock-climbing trip in Joshua Tree National Park, she huddled in the shade behind a boulder so she could interview for a job, also with Maine Huts and Trails.

Before long, the two met, hatched a plan to hike the Appalachian Trail together and finagled a way to work together at the same hut. Lindsay, for one, knew early on that she'd met someone special. You might even say her rubber chicken told her so.

"I was going to hike the AT alone, and I was kind of freaking out about it," she said. "I started asking anyone with legs if they'd do it with me."

Then, at a gathering of Maine Huts and Trails employees, she showed up with the rubber chicken that her family had given her as a gag Christmas gift, instructing her to take it with her on the trail, posing it for photos along the way.

"I was like, 'That's a great idea. I'll have a companion,'" she said. When she showed her chicken, which she named "Shengwey," to her co-workers, one of them seemed unimpressed. He walked away. A few minutes later, Mike returned with an action figure he'd taken on many of his own adventures and made a formal introduction.

Shengwey meet Wolverine.

"So that's when I knew I was going to marry him, and I started to figure out how to make that happen," Lindsay said. "That's when I started pushing the AT idea."

Mike, whose brother had hiked the trail a year earlier, said her invitation sounded good to him.

By the time they started hiking, the co-workers were officially a couple. Make that a couple facing a 2,180-mile walk in the woods.

"It was either going to work out horribly bad, or it was going to end perfectly," Mike said. "It just happened to work out perfectly."

After completing the AT, the couple began to work seasonally, spending the winters at jobs for Maine Huts and Trails, and winters in Alaska, where they worked at the upscale Kenai Fjords Glacier Lodge. That's where Mike became a chef's assistant responsible for appetizers, bread, desserts and the staff meal. Lindsay, meanwhile, headed up housekeeping. That experience proved invaluable, Mike said.

"I did learn a lot [at Maine Huts and Trails], but it wasn't the high-end stuff that I learned in Alaska," he said. "[Alaska] was the bulk of my training, where I got to work directly under a professionally trained chef."

Among the things he learned—how to make all kinds of wonderful bread. That knowledge fueled a passion that continues today. In fact, at Mt. Chase Lodge, Wednesday is "Bread Day," and Mike prepares loaves that he sells for five dollars apiece to a list of local subscribers.

"Bread Day" began as a promotion to get people interested in the lodge's offerings but has grown into a monster of its own. And pity upon the Downings if the bread isn't ready.

"One week we posted on Facebook that we weren't going to be around to bake bread, but we didn't call everybody [on the list]," Lindsay said. "It was a riot. People were showing up here, looking for their bread."

Lindsay said they won't make that mistake again. The couple was going to miss a bread delivery in August, but they let their customers know during the previous week's delivery and even included one of Mike's bread recipes for people to make themselves.

Another thing Mike learned in Alaska was the value of good desserts.

"I took a lot of pride in my bread and my desserts. I almost feel like they're the bookends of a meal," he said. "I care about the meal in between, but [breads and desserts] make people remember that it was a good meal."

At Mt. Chase Lodge, that ethos still stands. Luckily, the courses in the middle are just as impressive. On a recent visit, the beetroot sourdough bread and blueberry feta salad were followed by either a carne asada steak or salmon with a blueberry chutney, each served with roasted vegetables and either garlic rosemary mashed potatoes or wild rice. Dessert was a flourless chocolate cake.

All were excellent

In 2014, the couple was working at an Appalachian Mountain Club facility when Lindsay returned to Mt. Chase Lodge to visit her parents. The Hills had put the lodge on the market ten years earlier, but hadn't been able to sell it. Lindsay said she knew her parents were reluctant to ask if she and Mike were willing to purchase the place, but during one conversation the topic did come up.

"They started talking to me about how somebody mentioned that [we] might be interested in running this place," Lindsay said. "That's all it took, them taking that first step. It took a lot of guts for them to say that, because they never wanted to push anything on me."

Mike and Lindsay banked all the money they could over the next two years, met with business advisers and had an important discussion with Lucas St. Clair, whose family was working hard to establish a national park or monument nearby.

"When we met Lucas and we said, 'Hey, we'd kind of like to move up here. Is this national monument—at that point it was [being discussed as] a national park—going to happen? Because that's going to make or break our deal here,'" Lindsay said.

St. Clair's response convinced the couple they were making a good decision.

"That was the whole premise that gave us the confidence to do it," Lindsay said. "This area was going to be getting a ton of publicity, and people were going to be coming here."

Mt. Chase Lodge sits sixteen miles from the monument's north entrance and twenty-seven miles from the primary south portal. The couple have seen an increase in visitors since its official designation a year ago and are eager for what the future holds. To meet those new demands, they're working to improve their own offerings at Mt. Chase Lodge.

When the Downings took over operation of the lodge in February 2016, they knew they'd want to change things. One was a vivid reminder of the childhood Lindsay lived. The couple would not share their own living room with guests. Instead of sitting down in the lodge's main room to watch TV with guests, after meals are cleared and dishes done, Lindsay and Mike put a bell on the counter and retire to their own private quarters.

They've also changed focus. While hunters and anglers are welcome, they're not necessarily the target audience.

"When [my parents] were really doing well, it was because of hunting. They had bear hunters in here, and their hunting season was cranking," Lindsay said. "But hunters aren't really foodies. They want to be fed, sure. But they don't care, really, if it's the greatest salmon in the world."

Because cooking is one of Mike's strengths, the couple decided to focus on taking advantage of those skills in a way that few traditional sporting camps do. They invite the public to make reservations to dine at Mt. Chase Lodge along with the guests. Meals are served family-style, with one or two entree options and long tables that seat ten or twenty guests.

"We weren't basing it on any kind of model. I'd never been anyplace that did that," Lindsay said. "It was more of a way of making extra money."

And their modest financial goals were quickly surpassed.

"In our business plan, we estimated four thousand dollars a year on dinner by reservation. That's what we had to make," Lindsay said. "When we got here, word spread very quickly, and we did that in a month."

Not that offering the by-reservation service wasn't without some initial pitfalls.

"It was a little confusing at first, because we said we were a restaurant and had a sign [beside the road], and it said, 'Dining,'" Mike said. "Some people would show up and say, 'OK, we want to have dinner.' [I'd say] 'Well, typically we require two nights' [advance notice], but we can probably sneak you in.' They'd say, 'Good. Where's the menu?'"

The answer: There is none. You eat what everyone else is eating—while Mike will tinker in order to meet individual dietary restrictions. The reaction has been positive, once people figure out how the meal works. And while an increase in traveling customers will likely be on the horizon because of the nearby monument, right now the Downings are serving plenty of their neighbors.

"It's mostly really local," Lindsay said. Most of the people who come here are [from] Shin Pond, Patten. Occasionally we'll get people from Houlton."

And as the monument adds more infrastructure and becomes more well known, they're hoping to continue to improve. The couple has already tackled plenty of renovation projects, including adding new beds and refurbishing the porch off the dining room, which offers a beautiful waterfront view. More improvements are on tap, including a new furnace that will be installed for the popular snowmobile season.

And eventually, the couple might be able to take a day off.

"We'll be able to afford to pay help to help us," Lindsay said. "Well, that's the hope: To be able to have people to take some of the responsibility off our shoulders."

Laugh a Little

When I began writing outdoor columns full-time back in 2002, I had an interesting chat with our then executive editor, A. Mark Woodward. That position—outdoor columnist at the *Bangor Daily News*—had a bit of history behind it, with Bill Geaghan, then Bud Leavitt, then Tom Hennessey filling the role before me. In this biz, that's like playing left field for the Red Sox following three guys named Williams, Yaz and Rice.

I told Mark I was worried. If he was looking for an outdoor know-it-all, a truly experienced hunter and fisher, he was barking up the wrong tree—I wasn't that guy. If, however, he wanted someone who could laugh at himself and would likely make a few rookie mistakes while gathering stories that *Bangor Daily News* readers might enjoy, I might be his guy.

"There are too many outdoor writers who spend their time trying to tell readers how much they know, and how unattainable that level of knowledge is," Mark told me that day. "We want an everyman. Someone like you. Someone who'll make every mistake in the book and still smile about it."

That's what he got. And in the "be careful what you ask for" category, here are some of the results of that decision.

18. I Shouldn't Have Put on My Pants

For forty-seven years (save one humbling incident a decade ago), I was among the fortunate folks who experienced only a passing acquaintance with back pain. Friends, relatives, and co-workers complained about various back ailments for years. I tried to tell them I understood, that, as a former president might have said, "I feel your pain." But honestly, I didn't understand. Not a bit. Last Wednesday, that changed. Boy, did it change.

One moment, I was putting on my pants, preparing to head to work. The next, my lower back was in full spasm and I found myself on my belly, flat on the floor. But I'm a trooper. Or foolish. Or something. I had to get kids to school so I rallied and once I made it to the car (putting on socks and shoes took a little bit of help), I figured I might as well head to the office. It couldn't get any worse, I reasoned. Let me assure you, I soon learned I was wrong. Very wrong. And I can tell you exactly where that point finally took hold: On the office floor. Next to the printer. As a newsroom full of colleagues wondered if they should laugh, cry, or call an ambulance.

They settled on laughing.

Soon, my bosses sent me home. I'd like to think it was because I was in pain. Upon further review (as they say in the NFL), I realized I might have been ejected from the office because I told everyone within earshot that I wouldn't have been in this predicament if I'd simply chosen to show up at the office without pants.

I had, as far as I knew, history's first Putting-On-Pants injury. A quick note: In the news business, we are discouraged from referring to anything as "the first," lest we have to correct ourselves. Therefore, I wasn't particularly surprised, over the coming days, to learn that at least two other friends had indeed thrown out their backs the exact same way. The difference between them and me—they had enough sense not to broadcast their own Putting-On-Pants mishaps. Or to write a blog about it. And I didn't. Or don't.

On that Wednesday, it took three co-workers about twenty minutes to get me downstairs, into the parking lot, and into a car. They drove me home. I went to bed. And there I lay, for twenty hours. Eventually, I could stand. I could walk (as long as my strides were shorter than six inches). Finally I broke down and sought professional help. Now, a disclosure that I hope doesn't offend anybody: I am (or, more correctly, *was*) among those who didn't think highly of chiropractic medicine. I didn't disapprove of its existence, mind you, I just thought it wasn't for me.

After some spirited cajoling from my co-workers—so spirited, in fact, that I was fairly certain they were getting a back-cracker kickback—I finally agreed to seek help from a chiropractor that they'd had good luck with. After all, it wasn't as if I'd fallen off a roof or been hit by a car or had tried to haul a two hundred-pound deer out of the woods (if you know my deer-hunting history, you'll realize that I expect you to be laughing right now). I had put on my pants. And my back had rebelled.

So on Friday, I hobbled into a chiropractor's office. She quizzed me. She listened to my reservations. She put me on a table with too many moving parts, which alarmed me more than a little bit. Then she got to work.

Ten minutes later, I walked out of the office with a smile on my face. In full stride. With no pain. And today, after a second visit, she gave me a more-or-less clean bill of health. Just four days after I couldn't even get out of bed, I'm allowed to "resume all normal activities."

Skiing is allowed (though she cautioned against moguls). Running? Sure. But no matter what my new favorite medical professional says, there's still an activity that I'll tackle with great caution. I'd avoid it if I could. Alas, I can't.

For some reason, my bosses still demand that I wear pants to work.

19. Feeling Kind of Squirrelly

Golf is a miserable, fantastic, infuriating, and enlightening game. It can make grown men cry. I would have said grown men and women, but for some reason, it seems the only people who end up crying after four-putting from eight feet are us guys (and women say we're the ones who have a hard time expressing our feelings). In fact, I've found that golf has the unique ability to make men act like animals and to make animals act like golfers.

Confused? Good. That just means you're in the proper mindset for an odd tale.

I should have known something was up when my golfing buddy and I stumbled across a small herd of foxes (I know, foxes don't normally travel in herds, but like I said, this is an odd tale) at Bridgton Highlands Country Club. These foxes, three medium-sized critters who weren't noticeably foaming at the mouth, drooling, or looking at our legs like they belonged in a KFC value meal—put on quite a wrestling show on the backside of a green.

Odd. It got odder later in the day. After pulling a drive to the left edge of a fairway, stowing my club, and hopping into the cart, another guest arrived.

"Hey! Look at that!" I told my golfing buddy. "That red squirrel's looking at my ball!"

The squirrel looked up at us, grabbed the ball in his mouth, and beat feet for the forest. Little did he know that Golfing Buddy is not big on wildlife interfering with a round. He (Golfing Buddy, not the squirrel) dismounted the still-moving cart on the full gallop and gave chase while screaming: He told the ball-snatching vermin it was a low-life beast (the specifics are unmentionable in a family newspaper), said incredibly mean things about its father, mother, and siblings (ditto), and detailed what he would do if he ever caught the offending ball-hog (also unmentionable).

It all worked.

Moments later, Golfing Buddy emerged from the woods, triumphant, waving my Top-Flite.

"The little (expletive, expletive, expletive) saw me, dropped the ball, and ran up his tree," Buddy proudly told me.

But that's not where the tale ends (of course not, because if it did, this column wouldn't reach the bottom of the page).

A few weeks later, Golfing Buddy and I returned to Bridgton. When we got to the Squirrel Hole, I carefully aimed, fired, and watched my ball soar to a safe spot far away from Ballhog's domain. Trouble struck (as it so often does) on my second shot. I smoked a five-wood that ignored my instructions and flew into the woods on the squirrel-infested side of the fairway.

Luckily, I had a line on my ball, so I tromped bravely into the woods. I looked around and quickly spotted what had to be my wayward Top-Flite. At the bottom of a tree. Right next to four others. As I glanced around the forest floor, my eyes grew large. Everywhere—

under every tree, on every pile of moss—were golf balls. There had to be hundreds.

I had discovered Ballhog's stash.

I approached the first pile of balls like a lineman wading into an all-you-can eat buffet. I would gorge at the Titleist trough. I WOULD NEVER BUY ANOTHER GOLF BALL!

I picked up a ball. Examined it. And saw that Ballhog had chewed away nearly half the cover. The next ball? Also gnawed. And so was the next. Some featured just a nick. Others were chewed to the core. Somewhere in this pile of balls was mine. And I'd never find it.

As I trudged back up the hill to the fairway, pockets empty, I just knew Ballhog was out there, somewhere.

Laughing.

20. The Big Snip

I never knew. Honestly. I didn't. No matter what else you take from this column, please accept this premise: I never knew. Confused? (Apparently, I was, too). Read on and all the sad details will become perfectly clear.

It all started several weeks back, when Pudge the Wonderdog began whimpering every time he tried to jump up on the bed, or wobble downstairs, or when he slammed on his previously dependable brakes and tried to stop quickly.

A trip to the vet was in order. Pudge stood patiently as his doctor poked, prodded, and probed. After a few tests, it was determined that his prostate gland was too large. And as an eight-year-old INTACT (foreshadowing alert!) male, he had a problem that needed to be dealt with. At least, that's what the vet told me. After his prostate exam—an invasive, embarrassing proposition, whether you're man or beast—Pudge did not seem overly impressed with the doctor's . . . well . . . pedigree.

I could see his point. After all, it's not every day that you walk into a doctor's office with a limp and a whimper and find out that (even though it had nothing to do with your current malady) they're going to give you something to really whimper about. Lost in the shuffle: He's also getting a bit arthritic and has a narrowing of his spinal column (thus, apparently, the limping and whimpering).

The prostate, however, was the real concern. A simple prescription dealt with the limping and the whimpering—not a peep since—but that prostate? It needed help.

"He's an aging dog," our doc said. "And like aging humans (I may have imagined her raising an eyebrow, accusingly, toward me), the prostate becomes a concern."

The solution sounded simple enough. There were two problems, of course.

The first: Our doc mentioned "neutering" in front of the patient, a smart dog who, apparently, has read more canine medical texts than I have. The second? Well, I think we've already been there: I never knew. Not really. Not completely.

OK. Not at all.

Pudge, of course, did. He tried to put on a good face as the day of his surgery approached. He didn't limp around the house anymore. He didn't whimper. But as Karen and I discussed his appointment for what we called "The Big Snip," he seemed to be plotting. Apparently he knew what "The Big Snip" was. Even if I didn't.

Two days before surgery, he suffered a health setback that forced us to delay the appointment for a month or two. I'm not saying my dog is a liar, but I do believe that I saw him smirking as we walked out of the vet's office that day. He hadn't received a pardon, mind you. Just a stay. But that was good enough for him.

Eight weeks later, after more interesting health developments—I call them delaying tactics—Pudge was finally cleared for surgery. His appeals had run out. The Big Snip was a go. The neutering was on.

On the appointed day, I led a solemn springer spaniel into the vet's office, signed him in, and got a huge surprise.

"Yes. Pudge. For castration," the receptionist announced, loud enough for all the other dogs in the waiting room to hear. Pudge took it in stride. The other dogs may have wagged their heads in sympathy. Me? I recoiled. I know I did. As I said, I never knew. I really didn't.

The Big Snip, I got. Neutering? No problem. But castration? That, my friends, was a huge, huge deal, and somehow I made it through forty-six years on this planet without realizing that The Big Snip was a lot bigger than I'd always thought. Having known several friends and acquaintances who went through what I now think of as "the little snip," I figured the "neutering" procedure was similar. A little dog vasectomy. No problem. Not, for heaven's sake, a full-on castration. Never that. Nope.

One segment of my friends—male, non-dog owners, for the most part—admit (privately) that they shared my confusion. They might have thought the same thing, they say. Not that they'd have written a newspaper column about it, of course. Another segment—dog-owners and women—laugh aloud, quite certain that I must be kidding.

Alas, I'm not.

I'd tell you to go ask Pudge for confirmation, but unfortunately, we seem to have developed a bit of a trust issue lately, and he's not talking.

This, I fully understand.

21. Frogzilla

Over the weekend, I may have saved the Maine woods from a bloodthirsty beast named Frogzilla. At least, that's the way I choose to rationalize the fact that when I look in a mirror, the face staring back at me belongs to a mean old grump who ruined a nine-year-old boy's school vacation. But I'm getting ahead of myself.

Our tale of woe—or, if you prefer, our tale describing how a hero (me) saved the Maine woods—began last week when Karen took her three children on a nice vacation trip to an indoor water park in New Hampshire. During the trip to North Conway, more than a fair bit of shopping took place. And on one of their final stops, at a quite impressive toy store, nine-year-old Gordon found exactly what he never knew he'd always wanted—a grow-your-own frog kit.

What right-minded nine-year-old boy wouldn't want that? Heck, even I was impressed. According to the box, the frog—not yet named Frogzilla—would be quite impressive. It would be born in a laboratory. It would have whiskers. Its skin would be see-through. And if you were patient enough, you might—according to representatives of the frog factory—be able to teach it tricks.

Yes, Frogzilla would give you a high five. And it would even eat out of your hand. As a forty-something big kid who grew up reading comic books featuring ads that pitched the wonders of magical "just add water" sea monkeys, I was intrigued.

"His name is Sir Jumps-alot," Gordon told me, grinning.

A great name, I assured him. When I heard the rest of the story, I realized the Sir Jumps-alot saga might not turn out so well. The grow-a-frog kit doesn't really come with a frog, you see. Instead, you have to order your very own tadpole (Sir Squiggles-alot, I suppose), and you get to raise the little critter yourself. Still pretty cool.

Karen was a bit nervous. She had learned (after paying for the kit) that Sir Jumps-alot was from a long-lived species of frog. Some survive seven years. But the frog the toy store employees keep behind the checkout counter at the New Hampshire toy store? It was a gray-whiskered 23-year-old.

According to my quick math, that meant Gordon may well be thirty-two years old by the time Sir Jumps-alot met his maker. Even more alarming, it was possible I'd be enlisted as a part-time frog-sitter until I reached my seventieth birthday. Then I asked the question that ruined Gordon's vacation.

"Do you know if it's legal to have those kinds of frogs in Maine?" I ventured.

I explained to Gordon that Maine doesn't allow just any animal to live there. We talked about invasive species, and how some people set animals free in the wild, only to find out later that doing so had made things tough for the native critters. He seemed to understand. He also wanted to order his tadpole as soon as possible.

The Maine Department of Inland Fisheries and Wildlife maintains a list of unrestricted exotic animals on its website, and Karen got to work to find out if Sir Jumps-alot's adoption would be acceptable. All variety of critters are included. And like an exclusive party at a happening club, if you're not on the list, you don't get in. Six frog species were on the list.

Sir Jumpsalot, so far as we could figure out, was not. A bit more digging showed us that his particular species of frog may be particularly invasive. It may have been banned in at least eleven states. And it may be prone to eating its mates—and any other frog it encounters.

Simply put, if released into the wild, Sir Jumps-alot might morph into Frogzilla. Women and children would scream. Cities would topple. Civilization as we know it might well end. (Again, I'm rationalizing.)

Now, I write a lot of stories about invasive species. I regularly rail against those who stock illegal fish in our state's waters. And in the back of my mind, I could see the terrifying headline, in 72-point war type: "Maine Wardens Arrest BDN Outdoor Columnist for Harboring Invasive Froglike Beast."

Subhed: "You'd think he would have known better."

Fortunately for me (and, I keep telling myself, for the sake of Maine woods), I did know better. We didn't order the tadpole. Sir Jumps-alot will not be coming to Bangor.

One of these days—maybe when he turns twelve or fourteen—Gordon will even forgive me for ruining his school vacation by denying him the pet he never knew he'd always wanted.

22. How to Call Turkeys Like a Choking Cat

Knee-deep in camouflage gear and shotgun shells (with a rubber turkey decoy thrown in for good measure), I went about the prep work that would, I assumed, give me the best odds of success on Tuesday morning. I would rise early and dress like a tree. I would meet up with Hunting Buddy (who would also be dressed like a tree), sneak into the woods, and talk turkey. At morning's end, we planned to proudly

John Holyoke on a turkey hunt. Photo by Brian Feulner, Bangor Daily News.

cart our gobblers to the local tagging station, complete the required paperwork, and search the Internet for wild turkey recipes.

That was the plan, at least. As for my planning expertise, at this point it makes sense to admit I have limitations. Some might say I'm unrealistic, while I prefer the word "optimistic." Either way, we can all agree I have a hard time distinguishing between "bold-faced dreams," "wild-eyed wishes," and "reasonable plans." Not that any of that would stop Hunting Buddy and me from enjoying a grand old time on Tuesday, of course.

The first sign of trouble appeared on Saturday as I searched through camouflage hats, jackets, and trousers. For the uninitiated, if you plan to look like a fake tree, many ways exist to do so. In fact, manufacturers give their individual patterns cool names so the dress-like-a-shrub set can accessorize intelligently.

If, for instance, you're a Mossy Oak Break-Up guy (which, if you're looking for gift ideas, I am), it probably makes sense that all of you—from hat to boots—reflects that theme. I figure, if you're spending good money to blend in with the woods, the least you can do is make sure that you blend in with yourself.

Not that any of that worked, but I'm getting ahead of myself.

Back to Saturday. After finding, sorting, and choosing Tuesday's wardrobe—Mossy Oak Break-Up, as you might guess—I searched the house for my diaphragm turkey call. Picture a more flexible orthodontic retainer (without that cool wire wrapping around your teeth). In the mouth of a professional, that call can turn the most obstinate gobbler into a babbling, lovesick bird who will prance across the meadow, throwing caution to the wind, in an effort to find the source of that siren song. In the mouth of an amateur, the call emits a shrieking *blaaaat* that is more likely to send your dog running for cover and prompt your girlfriend to dial 9-1-1.

Trust me, I know of what I speak. After finding my call, I popped it into my mouth, puckered up, and gave it a little blat as I walked down the stairs. "Chock!" Just like the instructions said.

Karen met me at the foot of the stairs, a panicked look on her face.

"What was that?" she said, her eyes darting back and forth, looking for something.

"Urgey all," I grunted, not taking the call out of my mouth.

Karen's shoulders dropped, the panic passing. "Oh," she said. "I thought the cat was choking on something."

Cat. Choking. Hmm.

Come Tuesday, after a bit more practicing, I was ready to head afield. And while it may not seem so, I assure you that I had been training—for months, in fact—for the occasion. Turkey hunting takes place early. Really, really early. To sneak into the woods before Tom Turkey and all his pals wake and head to local bar in search of mates, we needed to get into the woods under the cover of darkness. The early worm gets the bird, or something like that.

Thankfully, for the past four months (ever since we started gaining hours of daylight, actually), my loyal springer spaniel, Pudge, had been steadfastly preparing me for turkey season. It was a gradual thing, thankfully. But Pudge, part-rooster, part-dog, wants—needs is probably not too strong a word—to start his day shortly after sunrise. He wants food. He wants to go out. He starts with a subtle nose-nuzzle. Then he whines. Eventually, he barks. Sleeping in is not an option. Back in January, my morning wakeup call came at 7:30. Now, the sun rises much earlier. Because of that, the daily dog-a-doodle-doo call has come at 5:45. Early. But not early enough.

Finally, on Tuesday, I got to give Pudge a taste of his own medicine. My alarm rang at 3:15. He opened one eye, as if to see if I was serious. I was. Reluctantly, or so it seemed, he stretched his legs and joined me downstairs. He ate. We went outside. And then I headed to the woods.

And the hunting? Well, as I mentioned, I'm an optimist, not a planner. As such, even when things don't turn out perfectly, I'm willing to focus on the positive. Hunting Buddy and I enjoyed an eventful day. We talked to at least three gobblers at first light (none of whom showed themselves). We talked to two more a couple hours later (neither of which would strut within shotgun range).

One turkey even turned toward us and seemed to consider coming closer. Closer to the decoys. Closer to our shotguns. Closer to the dinner plate. He eventually opted to continue his morning walk and headed off in the other direction. I don't speak fluent turkey, so I might be wrong, but I swear, as their retreating gobbles faded, I heard one say something about a choking cat.

23. Setting a Trap for Ted E. Bamster

When I began hunting, I paid close attention to the expert hunters I met, learned as much about animal behavior as I could, and knew, deep down, that the more knowledge I amassed, the more likely I was to be able to put it to use when I really needed it.

Last week, I needed it. Last week, I matched wits with Ted.

There's something you ought to know about Ted. He isn't a deer or a bear or a bird. He isn't even on the list of critters we Maine hunters (or trappers) even care about.

But Ted is wily. He is shrewd. He is (I learned) a foe worthy of respect. Ted is . . . um . . . a teddy bear hamster. My troubles began late one night, when Ted pulled his water bottle into the cage, hopped out through the resulting hole, and successfully staged a jailbreak the boys at Alcatraz would have appreciated.

Ted E. Bamster was on the lam. That's where I come in. As a licensed rifle-toting, blaze-orange-wearing outdoorsman, the other members of my household appointed me Head Hamster Hunter and told me I had to, somehow, some way, get Ted back. I laughed. *No sweat*, I thought. *I can do it*, I thought. *In an hour*, I thought.

Or not.

The problem, I quickly learned, was Ted had turned completely nocturnal (just like that big buck you tried to bag all last November). During daylight hours, he refused to come back to the food we offered. I crawled around in bedrooms, looking for clues. I picked up blankets and disrupted monstrous piles of stuffed animals, searching for any evidence of Ted.

No luck.

I gave Pudge, our bird dog-in-training, a crash course on hamster odor and let him have a go. Pudge crawled under blankets, disrupted monstrous piles of stuffed animals, then looked at me and (I think) shrugged his furry shoulders. So, it was on to Plan C.

I talked to co-workers and friends. They all had ideas and each thought my extra-special, gotta-work solution made absolutely no sense. Actually, I had two ideas.

One: Strap a tree stand to the wall and wait for the little varmint to return.

Two: Spread a thin layer of flour on the floor around our bait, then track him back to his ultra-secret lair.

A co-worker who had suffered through hamster jailbreaks of her own as a child suggested a large pot full of food, with a ramp leading to the edge of the abyss.

If Ted gets hungry enough, she said, he'll jump in and he won't be able to get back out.

Intrigued, I set up my own version of the trap, with a large cooler taking the place of the metal pot. (I told you this story was about trapping.)

Unfortunately for me (and fortunately for Ted), some unnamed people in the household began feeling sorry for their potentially starving hamster and put down a bowl of food—right next to my trap.

"He was hungry. And angry," I was told. "He kicked shavings all over the place and even spilled his water bowl to let us know he was mad."

"But we had him where we wanted him," I said, trying to avoid admitting that the mess had resulted when I inadvertently tripped over the assorted hamster gear spread over the bathroom floor. "He was hungry. He was trappable. And now he's full, fat, and happy."

The sad fact, I later learned, was that nobody in my house had any faith in my Cooler-Full-of-Chow trap, and everyone seemed to think Ted might be on the lam for a long, long time and shouldn't be forced to forage for his food. Beginning to boil, I launched Plan D, or was it E? I bought a live trap at a local feed store, slathered peanut butter on the tripping mechanism, threw a few peanuts on top (Ted is a nut for nuts) and put it next to my own cooler trap.

The next morning, I sneakily strode up the stairs to find the new, store-bought trap had been visited. Unfortunately, the trapper hadn't set it up right, and only one door closed when Ted came in for a snack. The result: Ted got two peanuts, then bolted out the open end.

On to Plan F: Reset the store-bought trap, then sweeten the bait in my cooler trap with an enormous pile of sunflower seeds. Ted is, I may not have mentioned, also quite a seed eater.

Finally, early Sunday morning, I had some honest-to-goodness success, the kind of success that grants the trapper bragging rights for months or maybe years. I'll let you know.

Ted's freedom was over. His hunger got the best of him. And there, knee deep in sunflower seeds at the bottom of the Cooler-Full-of-Chow, was Ted E. Bamster.

Off the lam. Finally. For now.

Last night, as I sat up reading just before bedtime, I heard an urgent scraping, rattling noise. I glanced at Ted's cage and saw him standing on his sleeping cube, pushing frantically at the roof of the cage. I chuckled. Well, briefly. Then I began to think. *He can't push the cover off that cage can he?* I wondered. *Probably not,* I allowed. *But maybe.*

So before turning in, I dropped one of Stephen King's more hefty volumes on top of Ted's abode, just to make sure.

24. The Mighty Kenduskeag Shows No Mercy

Over the forty-one-year existence of the Kenduskeag Stream Canoe Race, I'm happy to report, I have never flipped, nor flopped, at Six Mile Falls. I have not succumbed to "shopping cart hole." I have not asked for, nor accepted, any help from Dirigo Search and Rescue, the Bangor Police Department, or the local Cub Scouts. My Kenduskeag record, I'm proud to point out, is flawless.

The reason: When everyone else—452 boats-full, during Saturday's most recent April classic—heads to Mystic Tie Grange and starts packing on the pancakes, I don't. Instead, I head to Six Mile Falls, or Valley Avenue, lean against a tree, and wait for the broken canoes to start piling up. Pen and pad in hand, of course.

I would participate in your annual ritual. I'd love to get out there and show people the few whitewater skills I possess. But *(sigh)* I've got to work. At least that's my story. Most years, that's fine. And this year's race even gave the most bloodthirsty river vultures indigestion.

Broken boats. Fractured paddles. Soggy, despondent, abandoned racers, sitting on roadsides and riverbanks from Kenduskeag to Bangor, wondering where-in-heck their broken boats and fractured paddles had drifted off to. Not to mention, wondering how they'd ever get back to town.

I spoke with one woman I know (notice, I use the words "spoke with," instead of "interviewed," because if I'd tried the latter, she may have punched me) and she related a common tale of woe. She and her

Kenduskeag stream canoe race. Photo by Ashley L. Conti, Bangor Daily News.

paddling partner were doing fine, right up until they got to Vulture Central. Then everything went bad in a hurry.

She was still a bit waterlogged when I caught up with her, but she said her boat (and many important belongings) were last seen at Six Mile Falls, heading south at about 5 mph.

Since I'm a professional news man, I didn't laugh once. I laughed twice. OK, Three times. But after covering this race for so many years, I immediately felt badly. Her torment, I realized, was entirely my fault. If only I had written something, anything, to warn her about the unseen pitfalls beginning paddlers should avoid.

So, a day late and a few dollars short, here's my Veteran Vulture list of things for new paddlers to remember. Clip it. Save it. Laminate it (that part's important). And next year, sidle up to a new racer at the Mystic Tie Grange, and slide this list into their plate of pancakes:

Rule 1: Don't use your own boat. You just went up to Old Town Canoe and got a great bargain at the annual sale. You can't wait to try out your craft on the Kenduskeag. So you head to the village, paste a number on it, and . . . oops. Wrong answer. The Kenduskeag eats new canoes for breakfast. It regurgitates them just before lunch. And if you dare launch your shiny new boat, be prepared to be doing a bit of patching come sundown. If you're lucky. (See Rule 2).

Rule 2: Don't get too attached to your boat. A canoe or kayak is a tool. And if you've ever seen my personal filing system, tools sometimes get misplaced. Forever. The Kenduskeag gnaws boats, chews boats, swallows boats, and spits them up in places you'd never imagine. Your missing canoe? It might not be in Castine yet. Then again, it might. Or it might be in the woods of Kenduskeag. Or (if some evildoers found it) it might be on the top of someone else's truck. The race is 16 $^1/_2$ miles long. If you and your boat get separated, you may well find it . . . eventually . . . if you get help. Which leads to . . .

Rule 3: Write your name on your boat. In permanent marker. Several times. In locations that won't likely break, rot, or be dashed to bits by rocks. Add your phone number. Then, in huge letters, write this: PLEASE CALL ME! CASH REWARD! After that, hope for the best.

Rule 4: If it's electronic, leave it. Cell phones love water. Just ask my newly canoe-less friend. Hers was in a dry bag (theoretically, dry, at least), and after her mid-day swim, the phone stopped working. After drying out, the cellular beast woke up just long enough to taunt her a bit, and make her think everything was going to be OK. Then, an hour later, it rolled over and died for good. You don't need your phone. Trust me. Unless, well, read on.

Rule 5: About that other stuff. You can live without your wallet and your car keys, but you don't want to. The Kenduskeag gobbles up keys and cash, too. A couple years ago, a paddler told me that he'd fared well at Six Mile Falls. Almost. Made it almost to the top of the last drop. Then his canoe hit a rock, folded neatly around it, and everything in the boat was pinned by the unrelenting stream. Last I heard, he expected to wait a week, then come back to see if the river had spit up his boat. And his wallet. And his keys. Must have been a long walk home. Too bad he didn't have his cell phone.

Rule 6: Don't end up sitting around in the sun, or the snow. Make a plan detailing where to meet your pals at the finish. Then make another, potentially more useful plan—give all your valuables (especially the cell phone) to a loved one. Tell them that someway, somehow, you'll call and let them know where they can pick you up, should the angry stream steal your boat and disgorge you on shore in some inconvenient location.

Sounds unnecessary? On Saturday, the roads along the stream were littered with soggy former paddlers who were undoubtedly wondering how they'd ever get in touch with their loved ones or their boats again. Of course, that was all my fault.

My Kenduskeag record may still be flawless, but maybe I should have written something sooner.

25. Aren't Outboard Motors Great?

Outboard motors are terrific tools, and before I malign mine, I want you to pay particular attention those first five words, and the fact that I really, truly appreciate everything my motor has ever done for me. Like stranding me on Beech Hill Pond, forcing me to paddle a fourteen-foot boat to shore. Oops. Wrong list. But I think you get the point.

We anglers (at least those of us who aren't what you'd generally call "handy") have a love-hate relationship with our motors. When they work, we love them. Or, at the very least, we ignore them and forget that they exist. And when they don't, we write about them.

In the interest of full disclosure, I should probably point out that as far as I know, my four-horsepower Evinrude no longer hates me. But last summer, it did. Twice. And the year before that, it did. And a few years before that, it certainly did.

My own haphazard maintenance habits might have something to do with my motor's surly attitude, I suppose (if I took the time to make suppositions, which I won't, for obvious reasons). Instead, I'll just tell you this: At some point this summer, when I least expect it, my motor will hate me. Again.

Perhaps it will hate me because I ask it to push a fourteen-foot boat in the first place, knowing full well that I'd have a better chance of getting the old pork-barrel up on plane if I strapped on a pair of flippers and commenced to flipper-ing like a crazed loon. Perhaps it will hate me because I don't catch enough fish or because I ask it to troll long hours in the summer heat.

I guess I'll never know the answer.

But I do know this: The starter cord is getting frayed, as we speak (even though it's brand new). The gas is certainly going bad and fouling my plugs. The gas can is probably rusting, and the gas hose is probably cracking. And at some point this summer (most likely when I've got two fishing buddies lined up for a glorious weekend of trolling), it will somehow show me who's the boss. Not that there's ever been any doubt.

More than likely, my motor won't act up until I'm well out on the lake (a brief five-minute trip for a normal outboard, but a laborious half-hour belch-and-chug for mine). Then, it will burp once more and stop. If I try to restart it, the motor will gladly regurgitate its suddenly frayed starter cord into my lap.

Fix that, chummy, my motor will seem to say.

Since I'm a veteran of these outboard motor wars, I'll know exactly what to do, of course: Reach for the paddle and hope a kindly jet-skier throws me a rope before I get too tuckered out. And I won't be alone. One fishing buddy has an outboard that has started molting and is losing important parts (though he can't figure out why). Another pal is a bit tougher on the rigging and tends to run his outboard aground on shoals, deadheads, and other assorted debris. As you might expect, his outboard has taken to coming up with all kinds of assorted ills, none of which have anything to do with abuse he heaps upon it. Not directly, at least.

Despite all that, sometime this weekend, I'll be out there in my oversized boat with my undersized motor. (Note to motor: Sorry. You're not undersized. I just bought too large a boat for you.) I'll pile all my gear aboard and maybe a friend or two. I'll cross my fingers, pull the cord, and hope for the best. And maybe (motor willing) I'll go fishing. If I'm lucky.

I'll let you know how it all turns out.

26. A Thieving Beaver. Seriously.

Odd things happen to Nathan Baron. One of his teachers at Madawaska High School says this is true. Nathan himself admits it. Like the time he bought a new riding mower, put in a battery, cranked it up and watched, alarmed, as the battery exploded and his mower burst into flames.

"I thought I was going to die," he said with a chuckle. "I wasn't burnt or anything, but I was afraid I was going to light some trees on fire."

That teacher, Maine basketball legend Matt Rossignol, said that every time he sees Nathan, the teen has another story to tell. The one he told on Monday was particularly memorable, and Rossignol had an understandable reaction.

"I told him, 'We've got to get this in print,'" Rossignol said.

I agreed. Although at first I suspected the story was part of some school project titled "See What Kind of Crazy Story You Can Get a Newspaper to Print."

Nathan said this particular Saturday didn't start off as an extraordinary day. In fact, it was pretty low-key—he was sitting in a chair in the woods, hunting, watching as a doe crossed in front of him. After the doe left, he ate his lunch. Then nature called.

"I had to go to the bathroom but I had no toilet paper," he explained.

Luckily, he was hunting right across the road from his family's St. David home.

"I walked out of the woods and got on my four-wheeler and I went home," he said.

Another thing he did (which, for the record, we've got to advise everyone to avoid), he leaned his Remington .30-06 rifle against the tree, next to the chair he had been sitting in.

"And when I got back, I couldn't find the gun," he said.

Nathan said he stood up from his chair and began looking around in the woods. Then things got interesting in a hurry. Nature called again, but in a different way.

"There was a stream that was running about 100 feet away from me. I look, and there's a beaver hauling that gun into the water," he said.

Let's take a moment to let that sink in.

A beaver.

Stole.

His gun.

Nathan said he really didn't know what to do at that point.

"I was mad, but I started laughing because it was funny," he said. "I couldn't believe it was happening, that I was seeing him take my gun into the water."

So here's what Nathan did—absolutely nothing.

"There was nothing I could do," he said. "The gun was in the water and the beaver went under. That was it."

The water was deep, and pursuing the beaver was out of the question. The gun was gone. Besides that, the beaver was armed. OK. That was my concern. Nathan didn't mention it in our interview.

Nathan said he figures the beaver's intentions were more innocent. (So much for my image of a lone rogue beaver arming himself against trappers.) Instead, Nathan just thinks the gun was made of some good-looking wood, and Mr. Beaver decided to haul it home.

"He was probably going to go and use it as part of his shelter," he said. "Maybe I go there and there's a gun sticking up out of the beaver dam."

Nathan swears his story is true. Rossignol believes him. So do others. Things just seem to happen to Nathan Baron, after all. There are some doubters, though.

"My close friends don't believe me, but all the other kids in school believe me," he said.

And Nathan has a plan that he figures will convince everyone that his far-fetched tale is true.

"I'm trying to get my gun back," he said. "If there are beaver marks on it, I'm going to hang it on the wall of my garage."

27. Tick Magnet

I am, I have learned, a tick magnet. Let that sink in for a moment. Not, as we used to say back in the entirely inappropriate 1980s, a "chick magnet." *A tick magnet.*

That's not a good thing. And as you sit there, quivering with fear, revulsion and disgust, let me assure you that I'm feeling a little bit squirmy, too. Because once you start finding ticks crawling on your neck (yup) or your arm (yup), or perched on the sun visor in your car (more on that in a minute), every little mole, itch, and mild skin irritation instantly becomes a tick that needs immediate eradication.

First a disclaimer: I realize that ticks, and the diseases they spread, are serious business. I also realize that if I don't find a way to laugh my way out of these recent tick interactions, I'm going to lose it. So please, bear with me. My troubles really began a few years back, when I learned that the suburban ticks around my home were becoming bold. Every time I weeded the flowerbeds or spent any time outside, they'd hop on, hitch a ride inside, and dig in for a snack. Then, come three in the morning or so, I'd roll over in bed, feel the burn, and basically freak out.

I may or may not have actually scraped a tick-sized mole off my own skin in one such fit.

In the years since, ticks have become relentless as any outdoor activity is bound to stir up a few of the creepy-crawlies. Luckily, I've become super-aware (or, perhaps, ultra-squeamish), and I seem to have become adept at feeling their presence before they truly hunker down.

Of course, I may be fooling myself, and perhaps I'm not as adept at tick detection as I think. I am, after all, not small. And there are, after all, plenty of places on my south side that I might not be able to see, should a tick be lurking there. (I know, I know. Ignore the fact that you read this paragraph. It'll keep you up at night if you don't).

Luckily, all of the ticks mentioned in this column have been the not-so-threatening dog ticks, rather than the disease-carrying deer ticks. Not that they're any more endearing, of course. In any case, after about fifty tick-free years on this planet, the past half-dozen or so have become pretty eventful on the tick front. And recently, things got even worse.

It all started last week, when I spent one final day in the tick woods (oops. I meant to say "turkey woods") to spend one last day trying to find a bird. At the end of that fruitless session, I packed up my ground blind, my pack and my chair, and headed for home. Once there, I bailed out, locked up, and left my turkey-hunting gear in the car. Pro tip: If you're looking to make a tick terrarium, leaving a ground blind that has been out in the woods for a month in a warm vehicle for a few days is as good a method as any. Trust me.

On Sunday, after providing my tick community a couple of calm days to do whatever ticks do, I hopped back in my car, drove down the road, and immediately felt something ticky going on. Sure enough, one was marching across my hand. Later that day, also while driving, I felt one scurrying across my neck. Feeling itchy yet? Me too.

On Monday, shortly after I arrived at work, a colleague noticed a tick crawling on his clothing. Full disclosure: I had recently driven to the office and had just walked past his desk. For a day or so, I let him think that he was the tick magnet. Now I've got to face facts and admit that the little bugger probably just hopped off me onto him. Typhoid Mary's got nothing on me, apparently.

I thought that I'd grown somewhat blase about ticks, but on Tuesday, even I got a case of the heebie-jeebies. On the drive to work,

I noticed another tick, perched on the sun visor, just a convenient hop from my head. Taunting me. And finally, I admitted that I was the victim of a major infestation and needed to act. At lunchtime, I drove straight home, unloaded all of that hunting gear that had been harboring the critters (I hope), and washed my hands of the entire affair.

Of course, it wasn't so simple.

On my return trip to the office, I spied another tick—an especially bold one at that—clinging to the inside of passenger-side windshield, I guess that's the tick version of "riding shotgun." And now, here I sit, dreading the ride home. And going to sleep at night. And those phantom itches in the middle of the night. Again.

It's not easy being a tick magnet.

Gone Fishing

If you started at the beginning of this book, which is by no means a requirement, you understand that my definition of "outdoor columns" is different from many outdoor writers. Here, I'll try (kind of) to return to some sort of textbook definition of outdoor writing. Let's talk fishing! But while we're at it, let's talk fishing in a particular way. This section doesn't contain how-to or where-to information about the state's best fishing holes. I'm not going to tell you how to catch the trout of a lifetime. What I'll try to do is tell a few stories that resonate with you. Some will take you places that you'll want to experience for yourselves or will make you think, "Yes! I know a place like that."

Those places are special, whether the fish cooperate or not. We share wonderful times there and remember them long after we leave. Sure, we catch a few fish along the way. But more than that, we eat well, laugh a lot, and enjoy. And in the long run, that's why many of us go fishing in the first place.

28. My Old Fishing Vest

The ugly tan fly vest was there when I made my first tentative (and mostly futile) casts.

It was there when I caught my first fish on a fly and much later, when I caught my first on a fly that I'd tied myself. I was wearing that droopy mesh-and-nylon vest when my semi-frozen rod snapped on a 24-degree opening day. And the vest got drenched when I slipped on a rock and performed some impressive mid-river acrobatics in the East Outlet one hot July afternoon.

As long as I've been a fly-fisherman, which, as such things go, isn't too long at all, that vest has been with me. It held everything I thought I'd need but never did. And it held all the things I never thought I'd need and wound up needing time and time again.

Ugly? Perhaps. But only in a utilitarian, function-above-style kind of way. Zingers and forceps and floatant and nippers vied for space on the front. Each had its place. And in the heat of battle (or in the fading twilight of a glorious midsummer outing) I came to know exactly where to reach, which pocket to mine to find just the tool (or fly) for the job.

Today is opening day of fishing season. You may have guessed that. Or you may be heading fishing yourself. I'll be out there today. But somehow, it just won't be the same.

Years of use and abuse and weather and wind and errant hooks, along with dozens of drenching-and-drying sequences (most, for the record, due to my penchant for attracting freak rainstorms while fishing) have taken their toll. The vest that served me so well has been retired.

To most, that fact will not matter. To many, this discussion will seem absurd. But if you're one of us—if you've waded a wild river, determined to succeed (or fail) based purely on the magic you can coax out of a limber graphite rod and a vest-full of close-kept secrets—you may understand.

This vest held flies. It held leaders. It held strike indicators and bug dope. But it held far more than that. Somewhere in those deep Velcro pockets are all of my fly-fishing memories. Every time I've been fly fishing the vest was there.

Not any more.

Late last season, I knew the vest's time was running out. I knew I'd have to buy a newer model. Frankly, I loved that idea . . . at the time. After all, what would fly-fishing be without the endless supply of new-fangled, better-than-before devices (and vests) that keep hitting the market each year? The vest's old zippers were balky, the pockets worn, the D-rings threatening to let go.

It was time to trade up. And that's exactly what I did. Eagerly. I studied the new vests and compared prices. I tried some on. I looked at features. It didn't take long to figure out that my new vest—a not-nearly-so-ugly model—can hold things the old one couldn't. It will be more comfortable on opening day than the old one ever was.

Then a funny thing happened. Opening Day, that far-off notion that keeps snowbound anglers dreaming, and slaving away at the tying vise, got closer. It wasn't a far-off notion any longer. It was coming. Quickly. And I had to get ready. The other night, when nobody else was home to interrupt my reverie, I pulled the old vest out of the garage, and retrieved the new one from my bedroom closet. I placed them side by side and began transferring all the well-placed fishing gear from the old to the new.

With each pocket, the memories returned. Fly-shop price tags on the various products reminded me of those shops . . . the rivers and streams and lakes . . . the people I met . . . and meals I ate over campfires in remote places I hope to see again . . . soon.

The boxes of flies—each one opened and surveyed in turn—reminded me of the fish I caught and the ones I didn't. With each pocket, the memories continued. East Outlet. The Roach River. Sourdnahunk. Lac Barbel. The Hart Jaune. Shawmut. Solon. The Upsalquitch. Brown trout. Rainbows. Brook trout. Salmon. Bass.

As each fly box, each tool, each zinger, each roll of leader material was given a new home, I felt worse and worse. Everywhere I'd gone, the old vest had been. Every fish I'd caught, the vest had helped. Every time I'd bled, the vest had been my towel. Every time I'd needed a fly, the vest held it.

Sentimental drivel, I tried to convince myself. Then I grabbed another box and thought back to another trip. A special campfire. A special meal. A great day on the water. The vest was there for that, too. Maybe draped over the back of my chair or perhaps tossed in the bed of my truck. I wasn't paying much attention to those matters at the time. But I know it was there, somewhere.

That old, ugly vest has been retired. Sentimentality can't cure its ills. There was no getting around it. But I don't think I'll be tossing it in the trash anytime soon. The vest may not be able to carry all the fishing gear I think I need it to carry.

But it's still holding all those memories, and there's something to be said for that.

29. Bear Steaks and Brook Trout

With only one day remaining in our theoretical summer, an invitation to head north, leave paved roads behind, and sample some late-season fishing in Baxter State Park proved too enticing to pass up. According

Fishing on the West Branch of the Penobscot River with Mount Kathadin in the background. Photo by Brian Feulner, Bangor Daily News.

to the plan, guide Jay Robinson would lead us into a couple of remote ponds. The fish, he (more or less) guaranteed, would cooperate. And even if they didn't, we'd eat like kings.

If, that is, I agreed to bring along a bit of bear steak from my recently butchered bruin.

"I've never tried bear meat and am anxious to try it," Robinson confided in an email. "I was thinking a feed of those steaks might go over pretty good, cooked outdoors on one last trout-fishing trip in Baxter. I'd bring my Coleman stove, some of my garden vegetables, and hopefully a few fresh wild mushrooms picked along the way into another remote pond you've never been to."

As you may realize, that's the kind of offer you can't afford to pass up, and I didn't. Robinson is one of those guides whose fishing creed is pretty simple—If you're willing to wear out a bit of boot leather in your pursuit of good fishing, you're very likely to find it. And if you don't, on a given day, you're still very likely to have a pristine Baxter State Park pond all to yourself.

Up in "Katahdin Country," as Robinson calls it, it's still pretty easy to find places like that. All you have to do is look at a few maps and walk a few miles. Fortunately for us, many anglers subscribe to the easier-is-better school of thought, and don't feel like heading any farther afield than necessary.

"This is a good sign," Robinson said as we trudged over rocks and roots en route to one of his favorites. He stopped, brushed unseen debris off his face, and smiled.

"Cobwebs everywhere," he said. "I doubt anyone's been in here."

He was right. After hiking a mile or two, we reached a canoe he and his father, legendary Maine guide Wiggie Robinson, had stashed on the shores of the pond. As expected, we had the place to ourselves. The barest of ripples marred the perfect surface but did nothing to diminish the views of majestic OJI Mountain, Doubletop, and distant Katahdin.

"What do you think?" he asked, needlessly, it seemed.

"This is great," I said, as he knew I would. "This is great."

Shortly after that, Robinson paddled us from spot to spot as we slowly stalked rising trout. A few—including a sixteen-inch male in brilliant spawning colors—were lured to net. All but one—the "surf" in our previously planned rustic "surf-and-turf" feast—were quickly released.

A large bull moose called attention to himself with a grunt, then began drinking at the pond's edge. Our efforts to engage him in conversation failed, as the moose seemed to know that the calls emanating from the canoe had nothing to do with mating or moose. But he did stick around and made a slow half-hour of fishing much more enjoyable.

After the moose left, we headed ashore, laid out our supplies on a mossy, rough-hewn picnic table, and prepared to eat. The ensuing feast proved again that many times, the most satisfying meals are those you fix for yourself, miles from the nearest five-star restaurant.

"You know," Robinson reminded me as we began greedily chomping bear meat seconds after removing it from the pan, "Nothing we're eating came from a store."

Well, almost nothing.

The beans, cucumbers, green peppers, and tomatoes came from Robinson's garden. The chanterelle and shaggy mane mushrooms were picked a day earlier. Robinson caught the trout. I bagged the bear. The only "cheating" we did was relying on store-bought olive oil, garlic salt, and pepper. Forgivable sins, we figured.

After our late lunch, we decided we'd abandon the finicky fish in hopes of finding others at a nearby pond. A quick half-mile hike put us back on the water just as the breeze lulled, and as the sun began to set. On a small, glassy pond, the rings left by rising trout are obvious markers even non-guides like me can recognize.

Robinson again began stalking the trout, trying to figure out where a feeding fish would rise next. After five minutes, we found out. A fifteen-inch male, also sporting a bright orange belly, was lured to net and released. Though rises weren't constant, they were frequent enough that both of us refused to switch to heavier, sinking lines and continued to flick dry flies onto the surface of the glassy pond.

An hour later, with another fifteen-incher to our credit, we finally called it a day and began a silent twilight hike back to the truck. After sitting for several hours in a small canoe—and without the anticipation of a day of fishing driving us—the roots seemed bigger and the rocks more slippery than they had that morning.

But before we headed our separate ways, we made plans to head into the woods again soon. As long as I agreed to bring the bear meat. All in all, another memorable day spent in the Maine woods.

30. Someday

There was no shoulder-to-shoulder, opening-day crowd waiting on Monday morning, as we arrived at that special place in the Maine woods. Trucks were not parked two and three to a turnout, as they often are near the most productive pools. There was no line at the only store in town, nor anyone standing thigh-deep in the waters we'd come to fish. There was no changing of our initial game plan, nor moving on to another, hopefully less crowded, stretch of water.

There was only peace, quiet, and the presence of husky salmon that we knew lurked in the depths of pools we are often faced to share. These are the days that make it worthwhile, we figured. These are the days we remember, when the evenings grow cold and raw and spring is a distant memory, when fly fishing is a pursuit that will have to wait until snow ceases to fly and the lakes reluctantly give up their winter coats. Not because of the number of fish we catch, nor the size of them. But because every now and then—on those special days—months of talking and planning finally culminate in a fishing trip that isn't scrapped and isn't put off to another day. Put off to someday.

John Kirk is as avid a fisherman as you're likely to find. And over the past couple years, he and I have become friends largely because of that common bond. Over a drink or two at our local watering hole, the Winterport attorney has taught me plenty about a sport I thought I knew fairly well. And each time we talked, the conversation eventually

Dan Ryan of Ellsworth nets a salmon in Grand Lake Stream. By Gabor Degre, Bangor Daily News.

headed down the same wooded path: "We've got to go fishing at ..." he'd say, and I'd nod my agreement.

Someday.

For months, we had those conversations. We talked about flies I'd never heard of and places they'd work best. In our minds, we fished all of them, but in real life, we didn't. Not at the same time, at least. On Monday, we did.

The location doesn't matter. Not really. Chances are, you already know. Chances are, you've already been there. And even if you haven't, well, you have. Haven't you?

Each of us has a place like that, of course. The fishing wasn't great on Monday. But it was good enough. It didn't take Kirk long to show his expertise, tempting a bruiser (or so we thought) to take a nip at his "secret weapon." Alas, that fish tossed the fly before we got it to net.

We hopped from pool to pool, always arriving at the right time— No crowds awaited, no competition existed. In many of our most special places, like this one, that's not the case any longer. But on Monday, it was. And it was perfect.

The fish, to be honest, were a bit more finicky than we'd have liked. Especially galling (at the time) were the dozen or so fish we could see in one pool but which had no interest in anything we tossed their way. Over the course of the day, we caught a couple, missed several more.

And as our predetermined departure time came and went, we returned to the place we'd started, just to see if that bruiser, or his cousin, might show up for an encore.

He did.

That fish isn't the one we'll remember, though. At the local watering hole, I'm sure we'll talk more about the ones we didn't catch and what we'll do differently next time, on another special day in the Maine woods.

Someday.

31. Alvin Theriault and the Maple Syrup Fly

Out behind his fly shop, past the llama pen and the Icelandic sheep and the free-ranging, watchdog-wary guinea hens, bright red paint thoughtfully slathered onto a silo bears witness to Alvin Theriault's true passion.

Alvin Loves Connie

Women who come to Theriault's sprawling compound to buy his wife Connie's perennial flowers love the message, he says. Men shopping for fly-tying gear or materials? They're another story.

"The guys are like, 'What the hell did you do that for?'" Theriault said, chuckling.

To understand the reason, you've got to look a little bit closer at the family business—Theriault Flies—that sits on this hilltop just south of Patten. Look at all the birds, raised specifically for their particular genetic makeup and their ability to produce feathers that will produce the perfect fishing fly.

Look at the various other critters that are raised here, all, Theriault says, to produce fly-tying material.

Look inside the Theriault homestead, where tying materials of all shapes and sizes soak and sit and dry after tanning or dying. Deer tails here. Grouse and goose and duck skins there. Sometimes a foxtail or twenty.

"I pretty much take over the house," Alvin admits.

There was the time, he says, back when he was working as a game warden at Ripogenus Dam, when a local farmer dropped by and asked if he needed some calf hides for his tying business. Theriault did and the farmer proceeded to drop off a pickup truck full of them. The problem: They weren't hides, they were still whole calves, which had succumbed during a nasty winter. The farmer had been "storing" them on his manure pile. And they were frozen solid.

Theriault couldn't process and tan the hides frozen, so he did the only thing he could think of; he spread out a couple of plastic sheets in the kitchen and the living room and let the fragrant thawing process commence.

"So I'm a little hard to live with," Theriault said in a more-than-minor understatement.

All of a sudden, Alvin Theriault's silo love letter makes a bit more sense. Doesn't it?

"When you're making as many messes as I do in the house, you've got to do something," he said.

Messes, yes. But messes that fly tiers and fishers across the state, and beyond, have come to depend on. Since Theriault's retirement from the warden service in 1998, Theriault Flies has grown and is supplying at least twelve different stores with flies, selling other materials (with the help of neighbors Julie and Brian Johnston) via the Internet, and raising, processing, and selling more than one thousand birds a year, along with eggs to those looking to produce their own fly-tying feathers. He also finds time to tie 10,000 flies a year, including several thousand of a Maine favorite that he invented, the "maple syrup."

And Alvin Theriault wouldn't have it any other way.

He grew up in Fort Kent and says he fished more as a child than most people will in their entire lives. He'd leave in the morning, return at dark and spend the entire day on the water.

"My lunch was a bag of potato chips and a quart of soda," he said. "I loved to fish."

He also loved to trap—he worked his way through college by selling the pelts—and tie flies. The family farm was a potato farm, but like many others, the Theriaults generally had a cow or two, some pigs, and a flock of chickens. The chickens and rabbits were his responsibility.

By the time he was twelve, Alvin was tying flies. He began selling them at thirteen, and by fifteen, he was raising chickens to use in his tying. When he turned twenty-four, Theriault joined the Maine Warden Service and says he thoroughly enjoyed his twenty-year career.

But becoming a warden wasn't really his dream. Instead, it was the means to an end.

Alvin Theriault uses feathers from a variety of birds, including chickens, for his flies. Photo by Joshua Bright, Bangor Daily News.

"Most of the wardens, when they came on, that's what they always dreamed of was to be a game warden," Theriault said. "In my case, it was a really nice job, but I always wanted to run a fly shop."

And to do that, he knew he'd have to first work hard at a job that would allow him to retire early with a good benefits package.

"You can't make a living in this business," he said. "So I needed to have medical, and I needed to have a steady income, which the retirement gave me."

Connie ran the business when he was in the warden service. Retirement changed that.

Alvin Theriault wraps beige chenille on a maple syrup nymph at his fly-tying desk at his farm in Stacyville. The maple syrup is his signature fly and he sells more than 3,000 a year. Photo by Joshua Bright, Bangor Daily News.

"When I retired, my wife says, 'Well, the business is yours,' and moved on to [growing] flowers [and working at Baxter State Park]," Theriault said.

Ever since, Theriault has immersed himself in the business. The chickens clearly came first. The chicken barn was the first building completed on the compound, even before the homestead. Now, there are more buildings. Lots more. Some are house coops. Some are for breeding. Others are for storing processed fly-tying material.

And Theriault built them all.

"When we came here, there was an old house in a field with no driveways or anything," he said. "And I've been building ever since."

Now, he says, there are twenty-six buildings in the farm complex, he thinks. "At last count, there were," he said.

The tying and processing (he can dye materials nearly one hundred different colors) are only pieces of the business, though. The part Theriault keeps stressing is a bit more high-tech—he produces what he calls "genetic fly-tying" birds. Theriault keeps well-documented charts of each breeder bird he keeps and matches those hens with roosters he thinks will produce the kind of feathers fly-tiers want.

"We raise birds strictly for feathers. They are sorted for feathers," he said. "You're looking for long feathers. You're looking for stiff feathers for dry-fly fishing. And that's where the primary demand is."

Theriault's job is to supply that demand by rearing birds that give the tiers and anglers what they want and by improving every year.

"We're always trying to upgrade," he said. "That's what you're trying to do every year. You try to improve what you've got."

With a sixty-one-page catalog and shipments heading across the United States and Canada (and to tiers he buys from in Kenya), it seems he has succeeded on a grand scale. The only problem is that keeping track of inventory can be a bit of a chore.

"The biggest problem is trying to find it," he said. "I have people call and say, 'You got that?' and I'll say, 'Yeah. I've got it. I'm just not sure where it is.'"

Two things Theriault always keeps on hand—and knows where to find—are the materials he uses to tie his signature fly. In some circles of fishing buddies, the words "maple syrup" are whispered reverently and only when no infiltrators are present. The secret, however, is out: Most Maine anglers recognize the maple syrup as an essential part of their fly-fishing arsenal, and many others feel that on days when they're fishing still water with sinking line, no other fly is necessary.

How widespread is the fly? Consider this: Theriault says he sells about five hundred gray ghost flies a year, in a variety of styles. The gray ghost is another popular traditional Maine fly, and many fly fishers carry it.

But the demand for the maple syrup is off the chart.

"I sell over three thousand maple syrups [a year]," Theriault said. "And everybody's tying them. So that gives you an idea of how many are out there."

The fly's simplicity is one reason for its popularity with tiers and was a big reason Theriault began tying it.

"I was looking for something for my daughter to tie," Theriault said.

He met a man who was supplying a few local campgrounds with simple chenille-based flies, with no tails, and found that people were catching fish with them. He tinkered with the fly and spoke with Jack McPhee, a warden pilot and guide who was tying his own chenille fly. McPhee's creation was cream-colored with a mallard tail. Theriault branched out from that and created a fly consisting of yellow calf tail and beige—maple syrup-hued—chenille. And a legend was born.

Now he ties them weighted, cone-headed, bead-headed, and even flavored. And demand keeps on growing. The fly is simple enough that Holly Theriault (now a senior in college) mastered it quickly and became a commercial tier specializing in the pattern.

She was four years old at the time.

The secret, according to Alvin Theriault, isn't really the pattern, or the colors involved. It's the double-thick chenille and the size.

"We designed it to look like a worm, but at the same [time], size is really important to me, more than the color," he said. "It's the same size as the hellgrammite, the same size as the dragonfly nymph, it's the same size as the stonefly nymph, and it's the same size as the big green drake nymph."

The clincher, he maintains, may actually be the texture.

"A brook trout lives for what? Five years? So what type of entomology did they study?" he asked. "They didn't. They just grab [a fly] and spit it out. The thing with the maple syrup is, they probably don't grab it any more than any other pattern. They just don't release it because it feels good."

If that sounds a bit like fish-whispering to you, that's fine with Theriault. He, after all, invented the fly, and he and his devoted customers are the only ones who have to believe. Theriault definitely believes.

"I teach a fly-tying class in the winter. The very first fly we tie is the maple syrup," he said. "So, of course in the first five minutes everybody's tied their first fly, whether they've ever tied or not."

Then Theriault invariably asks a question.

"I say, 'I don't know what we're going to do for the next eight weeks, because you've already tied the best fly,'" he said with yet another laugh.

Theriault's plans for a fly shop didn't really turn out as he'd originally thought. At first, he thought he'd like to put his shop at the beginning of his long driveway, right next to Route 11. But a little matter of one thousand chickens (and other assorted material-in-progress) got in the way of that.

"I'd have to give up on the farm," Theriault said, explaining that he has an alarm system built in that alerts him when somebody drives into the yard, and he then stops tending the birds or beasts and heads back to the shop to unlock and service the customers. If he had to walk 200 or 300 yards every time a customer called—well, the birds might never get fed.

"You can hire someone to run [the shop], but it's not the same thing," he said. "Part of the fun of having my own fly shop is being able to be there."

Thus, the shop is the hub of his activity, not far from any of the barns or pens. As it is, tending the animals is already pretty time consuming, and potentially confusing.

"When I start feeding in the morning, so that I don't forget anybody, I start from one end and go around," he said, describing the circuit he takes. "It's easy to forget somebody."

And even though there are twenty-six (at last count) buildings already on the site, Theriault's got plenty more built, if only in his imagination.

"I have piles of lumber everywhere. I mean, I've got 10,000 board-feet of just boards over there," he said, gesturing to a nearby stack. "And I've got framing lumber everywhere.

"So I've got plans. But I can't seem to make the time to [build] any faster."

32. The Redneck Squire

One secret to writing about the outdoors is that it comes in handy if you know more than you're willing to admit you know. And it's downright deadly to know less than you're willing to assert in print. Make sense? It will.

Say, for example, that I go fishing and I know how to cast a fly expertly, and know where the fish live, and know what they'll be snacking on (If you read this space regularly, I realize this is getting far-fetched. Bear with me).

If I were actually to sit down and write such a thing, of course, two things would immediately take place. First, the fishing gods would look down upon me with great scorn and prove me wrong (and they might even make me slip on a rock and tumble downstream for a bit, just to prove a point). And second, one of you, somewhere, somehow, would be standing right there when I imbedded a fly in my forehead, or ended up catching a pine tree with four consecutive back casts, or failed to hook any finned critter whatsoever.

Then you'd never let me forget it.

Therefore, I have learned, it's simply safer to just say "I've got a lot to learn," and leave it at that. Even if my casting has improved. Even if my stream knowledge is getting better. And even if I'm catching more fish than I've ever caught in my life. When it comes to such matters, I have learned, it is best to listen to the sage advice of others who have been there, done that, and who are more than willing to tell me exactly what I don't even suspect, much less know.

"Holyoke, you're a neophyte," one such man told me last summer, as I sat in his camp and swapped tales after a long day of fishing.

That man, Jim Carter, owns Munsungan Hunting and Fishing Club. And he knows of what he speaks. In an outdoors world filled with well-read, opinionated, funny folks, Carter is (as I have mentioned before) one of a kind. He's that classic Maine combination: Profound/Profane or something like that. And for the record, I wasn't just "a neophyte." I was a blankety-blank neophyte. At least that's what Carter told me. And he's been around long enough to know.

John Kirk Rock. Photo by John Holyoke.

All of which brings us to this past weekend, when I realized (again) how much I've still got to learn and how much I hope that I never stop learning it.

The scene: East Outlet of the Kennebec River, a beautiful spot full of (we assumed) husky landlocked salmon. The fishing buddy: John Kirk of Winterport, a well-read outdoorsman whose own grandmother dubbed him "the redneck squire" many years ago.

On a thoroughly enjoyable day wading new parts of a river I thought I knew pretty well, Kirk showed me (again) what I didn't know. Yet. And he proved that when you're a redneck squire, there are plenty of ways to keep your secrets secreted.

His flies are pretty standard, I think. Complicating matters (or making things more interesting, perhaps) nearly everything he attaches to a leader has a nickname truly understood only by him and his fly-fishing buddies. For that matter, even his fly-fishing buddies have nicknames, culled from the Internet message boards that trade in such currency.

His pals include Streamer and Dropper and The Goat.

And his flies may be named The Cheeseburger, or Sponge Bob, or (no surprise here) The Secret Weapon. For all I know, he may even have a fly in his box named after you, if, that is, he's ever met you, and if your red hair is about the same shade as the marabou he used to tie it.

Kirk is not evasive about which flies are which. Not in the least. The problem is, after he tells you (or after he tells me, at least), it gets a little bit confusing.

Sponge Bob? Secret Weapon? What?

The one fly (or, more accurately, pair of flies that I've been really able to commit to memory is a streamer fly/nymph combo he calls "Why's-that-bug-chasing-that-fish?"

When the water's high, you need a "stick" to stay safe. That's a wading staff, by the way.

When you don't have a wading staff (perhaps because you're still a blankety-blank neophyte at heart), you do the "Do-si-do," whereby the non-neophyte links arms with the stickless sap and helps him across the troubled waters to the lie, seam, or riffle.

Then, you grab a Cheeseburger or a Secret Weapon or a Sponge Bob and get to work. I think. Of course, I may be wrong. I am, after all, still a work in progress.

And I wouldn't have it any other way.

33. Back in the Game

Even now, nearly eight years after an accident that forever changed his life, Philip Jandreau doesn't play the what-if game. You know: What if I'd done something differently? What if that tree stayed up for a second longer? What if I hadn't turned my back?

What if I could still move my legs?

Never played that game, Jandreau says—and you believe him. Never will, he tells you—and you believe that, too.

"I went to work in the woods that morning and probably around eight o'clock there was a tree I had cut [that] stayed up," Jandreau says, reliving the moment without emotion. "I was going back to the skidder and [the tree] fell off the hinge and caught me in the back."

Jandreau, then thirty-nine, a career logger from St. Francis, instantly knew the severity of his injury.

"I wasn't pinned, but I knew my back was broke. I knew that my legs, I didn't feel them," he says. "I knew I lost that, too."

Jandreau has told his tale countless times over the last seven and one half years. But over the weekend, his story took on new meaning for the scores of sportsmen who flocked to Aroostook County for The Fort Kent International Muskie Derby. The Derby has quickly grown over its three-year run, with 416 anglers entering this year's edition of the event.

After the event, when the dust finally settled and the sizeable cash prizes were handed out, there was Philip Jandreau, sitting in his wheelchair and telling his tale again—and grinning as a stream of well-wishers stopped to shake his hand.

"I'm probably working harder now than I was when I was walking," Jandreau says, offering a long list of chores that he performs for himself and others.

Jandreau remains paralyzed from his sternum down. But his backyard is his responsibility, and he mows and trims it himself. And those elderly ladies in town whose husbands have passed away? Jandreau takes care of their outdoor chores as well. Since his accident, Jandreau's fishing time had decreased dramatically, he says. Once or twice a year, his brother-in-law took him out in a boat for some spring fishing. And that was about it.

Until, that is, last August, when Jandreau bought a machine that made the woods and waters of Aroostook County accessible to him once again. That machine, a go-anywhere (more or less) six-wheeled amphibious ATV, is formally called an "Argo."

To Jandreau, it's more than that. To him, you might as well call that Argo "freedom."

On Saturday and Sunday, Jandreau drove his Argo over a steep bank and down into the St. John River and covered plenty of fish-filled waters in search of his first muskie. It didn't take him long; he caught a small fish Saturday morning and lost two larger ones. Then, on Sunday morning, he really hooked up, but discovered he had a small problem. The banks of the St. John River consisted largely of ledges in the place where he was fishing, and he had nowhere to land his Argo. He also had no net.

"I drifted down the river probably a thousand feet before I could find a place to come to shore," he says. "When I did, the fish was still active."

His son Jacob and Steve Pelletier were fishing nearby and came to shore to lend a hand. Two swipes of an undersized net were all it took to convince the fishermen that a new tactic was needed.

"Steve told Jake to grab it by the tail," Jandreau says.

That plan worked perfectly. A few hours later (after visiting Fort Kent to get the fish weighed and measured, and after rushing back to the river to try to catch a larger muskie), Jandreau sat in the crowd at "Muskie Central" and accepted the congratulations of dozens of other anglers and townsfolk. Some knew all about his 1999 accident. Others didn't. And everyone was smiling when Jandreau's name was called.

Jandreau didn't win the tournament with his 41½-inch fish. That's the reason he headed back to the St. John River after registering the muskie with derby personnel. But he did come in second and won $2,500 for his efforts. In a tournament marked by hit-or-miss fishing for theoretically plentiful critters, there were plenty of anglers who headed home without seeing anything resembling a muskie.

But there was Philip Jandreau, sitting proudly, having enjoyed one of the most successful weekends of all. Jandreau remembers his accident. He remembers the lessons it taught him. But he doesn't dwell on any of that. The future, after all, awaits. And that's all he can control.

"Just prior to [the accident] I'd had a divorce, and I had a hard time with it," he says. "I thought I had hit rock bottom back then, during the summer before I got hurt."

Unfortunately, that wasn't the case.

"When I got hurt, I had time to think and I said, 'Well, I guess I didn't hit rock bottom,'" he says. "But from that morning on, I didn't look back. It was just straight ahead."

34. Opening Day at Grand Lake Stream

By ordinary standards, Dave Huntress and Brian Foley were early risers on Tuesday morning. But judged differently—according to the time-honored tradition of opening-day anglers who flock to this fabled fishing hot spot, for instance—the two were nearly tardy. Across the state, open-water fishing season began Tuesday morning. At Grand Lake Stream, a sleepy, one-store, no-stoplight town in the middle of the Maine woods, that means that a long winter is over—almost. And getting to the famous Dam Pool early is a goal for many avid fly fishermen.

Note to Grand Lake Stream anglers: If you thought you smelled home fries cooking while you were wading early Tuesday morning, you didn't. Really. You didn't. You smelled Foley. More accurately, you smelled Foley's car, a well-worn Mercedes sedan that has been retrofitted to burn used vegetable oil as well as diesel fuel.

After leaving Orono at around four in the morning, Foley and Huntress burned some serious fat and pulled the veggie-mobile into the slushy parking lot early (for us) but late (for them).

"We got here late for opening day," Foley said with a grin. "We pulled up at six thirty. Normally we're here just when it's light enough to begin casting."

The veteran anglers wasted no time in getting down to business: By ten, Huntress had hooked and released six landlocked salmon. Foley had caught and released two more. They'd also taken some time to hop out of the frigid water and visit the Pine Tree Store, which serves as the town's clearinghouse of opening-day information.

Huntress said he could wade for about two hours without taking a break to warm up. "But I'm nuts," he said. Huntress admitted that he might have been able to stay in the water longer, except for one small equipment malfunction.

"That hole in my waders that was there two years ago is still there, in my right foot," he said. "But other than that, I'm doing pretty good."

Kurt Cressey, the good-natured proprietor of the Pine Tree Store, said that in Grand Lake Stream, cold opening-day conditions serve an important purpose. On days when the fishing is good, freezing fingers and toes offer further encouragement for anglers to share the good fishing spots with others.

"When the water is thirty-two degrees, there's no problem with rotation" [in and out out of the busy Dam Pool], Cressey said.

As you might expect, the water flowing out of nearly ice-covered West Grand Lake was a bit nippy. But the day's weather was a pleasant surprise for some anglers. The wind didn't blow, and temperatures hovered around forty degrees. Balmy? No. Fishable? Sure.

A few inches of overnight snow and slush turned the Dam Pool parking lot into a mucky mess, and some anglers sat down and slid gingerly down the stream bank to avoid embarrassing splashdowns while getting to the water. Still, nobody was complaining.

It was, after all, opening day.

"This is milder than usual opening-day weather," said Foley, who has eleven straight Grand Lake Stream openers under his belt. "It's not as warm as they said it was going to be, but it's bearable. It's not raining. It's not sleeting. No ice in the guides [of the fly rod]. So we're doing OK."

The weekday opener and high gasoline prices (for those not driving modified veggie-mobiles) probably kept the crowd down a bit, so it was easy to find a spot in the usually packed Dam Pool. Some years, twenty or more anglers vie for position in the pool on opening day. On Tuesday, only eight fished at once during the busiest times, Foley said.

And the fishing? Huntress had no complaints.

"I didn't expect the fishing to be as good as it is today," He said. "Everybody, looking around the pool, has been getting into fish. It hasn't just been one or two spots. People have been catching fish all around the pool."

In Grand Lake Stream, tales of fishing success (or failure) always work their way uphill, sooner or later. That means Cressey, whose store is perched on the bank of the stream, ends up with plenty of stories to share with the anglers who stop by to take advantage of the free opening-day coffee or to rest on the popular liar's bench.

John Holyoke and other fishermen vie for position in the Dam Pool at Grand Lake Stream on opening day of open water fishing. Photo by Gabor Degre, Bangor Daily News.

Fly box. Photo by John Holyoke.

"There are a couple of guys who have already caught their eighteen salmon up in the Dam Pool," Cressey said, not long before noon. "Now they're going downstream to see if there's any [fish] in the Hatchery Pool or maybe Little Falls."

Year after year, anglers target Grand Lake Stream as their opening-day destination, and year after year, they get what they came for. What that is can vary.

"I think people have to get it out of their system and basically go fishing," Cressey said, pointing out that after a long winter, fly fishers are eager to dig out their equipment and work out the kinks.

"This is one of my favorite places on opening day. There's always the variability of whether or not you're going to find fish," Huntress said. "This year, because of the flows, it has been nice. There's a lot of fresh fish and a lot of real fat fish this year."

Domtar, which controls the dam at Grand Lake Stream, ran fairly high water into the stream leading up to opening day, but reduced those flows Monday and Tuesday to provide better wading conditions. Foley said knowing he has a good chance to catch a salmon is one thing that draws him back year after year—but that's not the only thing.

"More than anything, I think it's just the camaraderie and the tradition," he said. "It's just an opening-day ritual, really."

For the anglers, to be sure. But for the local storekeeper, too.

"The swallows come back to Capistrano, and the salmon come back to Grand Lake Stream," Cressey said.

Some of those fish do return to Grand Lake Stream. Others live in the stream all winter.

Either way, when the season opens, the anglers will be there, and after a long, harsh winter, Cressey will be smiling. This year, that may be even more true than in years past. Just take a look at the picture window of the Pine Tree Store, and you'll find all the evidence you'll need. The display isn't full of fishing gear, nor ice fishing equipment, like it often is. In January, Kathy Cressey, who owns and runs the store with her husband, decorated the window in a tropical theme, complete with pink flamingos.

"So we sit around and sing Kumbaya," Kurt Cressey said with a grin. "You can tell we're getting a little squirrelly. It's been a long winter."

35. Perfect Timing

For years the tiny, meandering brook has been a topic of discussion, the possible source of many adventures, none of which, unfortunately, have been realized.

"We've just got to hit it at the right time," my fishing pals and I told each other, year after year. "Early. You know. Right after the alder leaves get as big as a mouse's ear, just like the old-timers tell you."

Those conversations, of course, always occur in July or August or during hunting season in November, as we stalked deer along the same stream. We'd nod our heads, agree that hitting that particular brook in early May (when those alder leaves reach a certain, special size, of course) would lead us straight to trout city. In a stream like that, we reasoned, brookies must live around every corner. They must thrive in every pool. They must. They must. If only we could remember to be on the water at the right time. Last weekend, after forty-four years traveling across a bridge that spans that tiny brook, I did. Finally.

To make the day even more special, I had a young, first-time trout fisherman with me. Together, we made a few stops on the way to the fishing grounds. A large store for a special lure. A convenience store for essentials such as juice, soda, chips, and worms. Another shop to buy a couple of sandwiches, which we'd eat in the truck before beginning our ambitious hike.

The conditions, we learned, were perfect. The water flow was good. Black flies had begun to gather but weren't yet biting so a bit of bug dope sent the message to the swarm. We chatted with a couple of anglers at the trailhead and learned that they'd had some luck.

My eight-year-old fishing buddy was enthused. So was I. Into the woods we went. Past the beaver flowage. Around (and sometimes through) the mud and the muck. Up hills. Over rocks. And finally, we reached the spot my pals and I always knew would produce fish. If we were there at the right time. If the conditions were right.

"See this alder tree?" I asked my fishing partner. "These leaves are as big as ..."

"A mouse's ear!" he finished.

Yes, they were.

At the first few spots, we had no luck. The pools looked good, but the trout weren't there or weren't interested.

"I'm getting bored," my fishing buddy said. "Can we go back?"

I'd expected as much. Our past fishing experiences had come in more controlled environments. We'd fished out of a boat, over a rock where sunfish are plentiful, hungry, and not too discriminatory. Making the transition to fishing for finicky brook trout, I knew, might be a challenge. As the self-appointed guide, I decided to push on, at least for a few more minutes.

"Not quite yet. We're just getting to the best spot on the stream," I told him, not quite knowing if the pool ahead was any better than the ones we'd already fished, but hoping for the best.

One trout. Just give us one trout.

After one drift of the worm-enhanced lure, we got a rise. I prepared to replicate the previous drift and announced our plan.

"I'm casting to that rock on the other bank. I'm going to hand the rod to you. And you're going to catch that fish," I said.

"Are you sure?"

"I'm sure."

Thankfully, I was right. I flipped the lure to the deep water. Handed over the rod. And the trout darted out from his hiding spot and grabbed his meal. My smile, I imagine, was broad. My fishing buddy's grin was probably even larger, his eyes wide as he brought his first-ever brook trout to hand.

"What do you want to do?" I asked. "You can eat him if you want. Or we can let him go."

We'd already talked about ethics on the way to the stream. We'd talked about catch-and-release, about leaving fish for others to catch, but also about how tasty brook trout are.

"This time, I think we ought to let him go," my fishing buddy said.

"Sounds good to me," I replied. "Sounds good."

Shortly after that, we both decided we'd had enough adventure for one day. We had hiked. We (or one of us, at least) had fallen into the stream. We had gotten muddy and sweaty. We even caught a trout. To me, that's a pretty complete day on a trout stream. As we arrived back at the truck and stowed our gear, my fishing partner looked skyward and frowned.

"Did you feel what I just felt?" he asked.

"A raindrop," I agreed. "Looks like you picked the perfect time to turn back after all."

"Yeah," he agreed. "I guess I did."

On the Hunt

Before we begin this section, I must confess something. Although I'm an avid deer *hunter,* I'm apparently a lousy deer *shooter.* I have yet to fill my deer tag in my seventeen years of trying. If that makes you want to ignore this section, I'm sorry to hear that. But if you've gotten this far, hopefully you'll stick around, waiting for a surprise or two.

While I have struck out on deer, I have, however, shot a couple of moose, and my buddies and I regularly stage what we call catch-and-release moose hunts during those years when none of our names are drawn for coveted moose permits. And I love to walk behind my tiny English cocker spaniel, waiting to see if he'll find a grouse or woodcock for me to miss.

But, as you may have learned by now, these stories are special to me not because of what was shot, or the wild game that was harvested, but because of the places and people and the memories made.

36. The Old Pats Society

Bill Hamilton grinned at the question, his stock answer already halfway out of his mouth. "He's an English setter," Hamilton said, setting up the

Pete Warner and Chris Lander flank Teddy (John Holyoke's English Cocker Spaniel), while bird hunting hear Brassua Lake. Photo by John Holyoke.

punch line as he prepared nine-year-old Woody for another enjoyable day afield. "He is the only kind of bird dog there is."

Hamilton later allowed that he was joking, more or less. But on a day spent tromping through grouse and woodcock coverts, Woody certainly lived up to his owner's assessment of the breed and deserved the praise others heaped on him dog when the guide wasn't within earshot.

"You may never hunt behind a better bird dog. Ever." That's what many members of Old Pats Society will tell you, when they're sitting around, swapping tales. They use words like "fantastic," "unbelievable," and "world class."

Coming from members of the Old Pats Society, that's high praise. This group of well-traveled friends (along with several invited guests) returned to Forest City recently for a weeklong outing hosted by Art and Doris Wheaton and Lance and Georgie Wheaton of The Village Camps. Birds were flushed and shot (or not). Yarns were spun. Friendships were renewed. New memories were made.

Just ask Chris Dolnack.

Dolnack, an invited guest from Suffield Connecticut, who serves as senior vice president of the National Shooting Sports Foundation, spent a glorious Wednesday with Hamilton and his dogs and did exactly what he'd hoped to do. He continued a tradition.

In the company of men who take their shooting sports (and their shotguns) seriously, Dolnack spent the day toting a gun that was special not because of its pedigree or its monetary value but because of its origin.

"This was my grandfather's meat gun, I think the only shotgun he owned," he said during an afternoon break. "It's a Savage Stevens Model 5100, 16-gauge."

In a special place, working behind a dog some describe as legendary, it seemed to be the perfect occasion to run the old Savage through its paces.

"He carried it for fifty years and the gun was passed along to me," Dolnack said. "I recently got it checked out by a competent gunsmith to make sure it was safe to use, and came up here to try to bag something with granddad's gun so that I can pass it along to my kids or maybe my nephews."

Though Dolnack isn't an Old Pat—attaining membership in the group is difficult—he obviously shares the group's sentiments. The Old Pats are big on tradition, nostalgia, and preserving a way of life that isn't as common as it once was.

"I think that's what's so great about our hunting heritage," Dolnack said, after bagging three woodcock with his grandfather's old gun. "One generation passing on woodsmanship and ethics and marksmanship and conservation ethic to the next generation."

Dolnack may have shot a limit of woodcock, but if he hadn't, he wouldn't have worried about it. Neither would any of the Pats. Those days, member Art Wheaton says, are over.

"It's not important to us whether we limit out, whether we kill a lot of birds," Art Wheaton said. "If we make some good shots and kill a bird here or there, it's frosting on the cake. We just have a good time."

All around him on Wednesday night on East Grand Lake, as a bluegrass band played and steaks were served at Wheaton's beautiful log home, similar sentiments were shared by men who sometimes worked together, often hunted together, and who have shared a lifelong passion for the outdoors.

"This is what the tradition of hunting and sports shooting and firearms ownership is all about, as far as I'm concerned," said James Jay Baker. "These kinds of get-togethers have been going on since the first people arrived on these shores from wherever they were from, and probably before that. I'm sure the Indians had the same sort of camaraderie."

Baker, an Old Pats member, knows the shooting sports well. He spent twenty years working for the National Rifle Association (NRA), and now works as a partner for the Federalist Group in Washington, D.C.

"[This reunion] is very special. You can see it's not about killing as many birds as you can or anything like that," Baker said. "It's about the camaraderie, the shared tradition, the fellowship, just being in each others' company, and swapping a few lies and maybe having an adult beverage or two."

Tradition. Camaraderie. Again and again, those key concepts are discussed. Pass it along to the next generation. Enjoy the time you have. Live. Laugh, and sometimes get laughed at. It's all the Old Pats way.

Guns brought many members of the society together, and guns still help cement that bond today. Art Wheaton and many other members worked at Remington Arms. Several are also passionate about Parker shotguns, and their annual gun show is a key part of the Old Pats Society outing. Although they love collecting Parkers, they realize that sharing the tradition of those fine American-made firearms is a responsibility they can't ignore.

A few years back, Art Wheaton illustrated that when he gave away his favorite Parker, a gun he still calls "a grouse machine." At an Old Pats Society outing, he handed the gun to his son, Shane, during a special ceremony.

"It was important for me to give it to him while I was alive, so he could enjoy it," Art Wheaton said. "It was more important for him to have my gun than it was for me to kill a lot more grouse."

Charlie Herzog, a tireless retiree from Ste. Genevieve, Missouri, is another Parker buff. During his stay in Forest City, Herzog—a member of the board of directors of the Parker Gun Collectors Association— was in the middle of all the festivities. If there was dancing to be done,

Herzog did it. If there were jokes to be told, Herzog told them. And if there were new friends to be made, Herzog was the one-man welcoming committee even though he, too, was an invited guest, not an official Pat. Spend time with him in a bird covert and he'd keep you laughing. Ask him about Parker shotguns and you'd get an enthusiastic earful.

→ "Artwork is not necessarily canvas and oil," Herzog said. "It can be wood and steel. And a lot of these old firearms that folks like to hunt, collect, and appreciate are just like that: They're works of art."

Herzog was bitten by the Parker bug thirteen or fourteen years ago, he says. Since then, he has owned several. The hunt, he says, is more important than the acquisition. And the people make it all worthwhile.

"You have lots of history, lots of nostalgia, and lots of fun," Herzog said. "And you meet some wonderful people. Those are the kinds of things that make it fun."

Herzog, you quickly realize, is not a man who ever lacks for fun. Those around him end up chuckling, or smiling, or nodding their heads. This camaraderie thing? Herzog's a world-class practitioner of the craft. All of which suits Art Wheaton perfectly. Hunting and shooting have been a big part of Wheaton's life. But the little things remain important. Spending time around the people who can appreciate those little things is more of a focus as the years pass.

"There is a beginning and an end, and we're all closer to the end than we are to the beginning," Art Wheaton said. "I've said it a dozen times to this crowd: We've got more grouse hunts behind us than we do in front of us."

Wheaton paused and smiled. Steaks were on the grill. The strains of bluegrass music wafted onto the deck. Life was good.

"It's important for us to pass this along to our kids," he said, sharing the message of the day. "That's what it's all about."

37. Moose Hunt at Cassidy Deadwater

When you're planning "the hunt of a lifetime," as Maine wildlife officials like to call it, a few things are essential. Food, for instance. Lots and lots of food. And friends (who may or may not have any real hunting expertise, but who are willing to pitch in, laugh at bad jokes, and add to the general moose-camp atmosphere).

You've got to have a plan, and (as we all found out) be willing to change it. That was the case this week, as my moose-hunting party headed into the woods for my own hunt of a lifetime.

Meeting the characters (a word which defines them in a variety of ways), I suppose, is the first order of business. The Lander boys are born hunters who truly know their way around the woods of Maine. For the record, the Lander boys are also exceptionally unlucky when it comes to moose-permit lotteries, and despite entering for the past twenty-six years, none has ever had his name pop out of the state's electronic hopper.

Not Chris, my sub-permittee, who learned his woodscraft from his father, Bill, and his brothers. Not Billy, who lives in Dedham, nor Timmy, who resides in Eddington. But on Sunday, thankfully, they were there, loading trucks and heading northwest along the Golden Road to our hunting grounds near the Cassidy Deadwater, located seven miles north of Northeast Carry, which is at the northern tip of Moosehead Lake.

Pete Warner, a fellow writer at the *Bangor Daily News*, tagged along for moral support (and, as he'd tell you, comic relief). He doesn't hunt . . . yet. We're working on that.

Mark Kingsbury of Dedham is one of the owners of the camp we stayed in, and he came along for the ride, and to share his knowledge of the area. Bridget Brown, a *Bangor Daily News* photographer who was assigned to document the expedition, and quickly became a vital part of the team, rounded out our group.

On Sunday, we loaded up two weeks worth of food, a couple firearms, a magic digital game call, and other sundry supplies, and headed into the woods for what might be a one-day journey or might stretch on for days. And we did have plans. Shoot a moose. Get a story. Eat too much. Laugh. Live. Learn. And most importantly, enjoy the moment, regardless of how long that moment takes.

Wish us luck. It could get interesting.

Cassidy Deadwater is beautiful, in that desolate, murky, moosey way that seems to exist only in the T-whatever, R-something-or-other locales where moose hang out. Old timber operations are evident, if you look hard, because most of those former clearcuts have since grown into thick stands of moose-hiding alders, or parcels consisting of spruce and hardwood.

Our base camp, which was built in 1993, sits high on a ledge overlooking the deadwater. It's a perfect place, one would think, to spy a moose or something else. And it is. Not an hour after unpacking three truckloads of gear and supplies, Brown made the transition from "photographer" to participant.

"What's that over there?" she asked, pointing at a distant shore, a mile or more away.

A stump, we figured.

"But it's moving," she told us.

It was moving. And after scrambling for binoculars, we found that moving stump was a monstrous bull moose. Kingsbury smiled and told us he knew a road that would take us near that bull's location. We would hunt it the next morning. *And the hunt will be over,* I thought.

Mark Kingsbury (left), Tim Lander, and Bill Lander grabbing some food at Kingsbury's camp near the Cassidy Deadwater. Photo by Bridget Brown, Bangor Daily News.

This will be easy. That's what I thought, anyway. But the moose, it turned out, had his own plan.

At this point, it's important to note one critical fact—I didn't really want the hunt to end Monday. Honest. My reasons were purely selfish. The saga of a five-minute moose hunt, I figure, wouldn't fill much newsprint and we were, after all, looking for a tale to tell.

Tuesday would be better, Wednesday ideal. That's my story, anyway.

Encouraged at Brown's moose-spotting effort, we ate pan-fried spaghetti carbonara (I know, that's not the way Emeril would prepare it, but I was the chef and had a hard time thawing out my masterpiece). Not long after, one by one, we began heading to bed.

A moose awaited. *Our* moose awaited. The hunt was upon us. It was time to get down to business.

Moose hunters go about their work in different ways. Some prefer what they call "traditional hunts," and take a canoe into the wilderness,

Bill Lander, Peter Warner, John Holyoke, Tim Lander, and Chris Lander. Photo by Bridget Brown, Bangor Daily News.

packing the moose out after quartering it. Others like to drive the roads, checking out clearcuts and bogs for their quarry.

And others, like us, begin our hunt with a plan to hit likely spots, set up, and call the moose to us. Old-time moose hunters did their calling with birch-bark megaphones, through which they bellowed like a bull, moaned like a cow, and (hopefully) lured a moose within range. Many still use that tactic.

My moose-calling skills are still rudimentary, and my best efforts probably sound more like the screams of a skunk with a head cold than a moose of any size, shape, or gender. That's where Peter Brown comes in. Brown, who went to Brewer High School and Maine Maritime

Academy in Castine, is a co-founder of Hampden-based Extreme Dimension Wildlife Calls.

We had one of his Phantom Pro-Series calls, and all of us were eager to give it a try.

For the record, most of us were so eager we took turns firing off salvos of moose noise on the digital wonder while we were still sitting in camp. It didn't take long for the Phantom to pay dividends—almost.

Standing in the woods along an old timber-harvesting road on Monday morning, Kingsbury set up the call and began pushing buttons. From the direction of a nearby stream, the answering calls of a lovesick bull began. It was distant at first . . . but then grew closer . . . and closer.

Then they stopped. For a half-hour, we waited. No grunts. No bellows. Nothing. The moose, it seemed, had figured us out. Discouraged, we unloaded our weapons and hopped back in the truck. Bad idea. Two hundred yards up the road, we met Mr. Moose. Our intrepid photographer swears it was the same bull she spied Sunday night. And he didn't plan on hanging around to gauge our intentions. A few seconds later, as Chris Lander and I performed a less-than-graceful dismount from the truck, the moose disappeared into the woods.

"I guess that shows the importance of patience," Kingsbury told us.

The rest of the day featured more of the same. Much more. Other moose wanted to talk to us about our hunt, but they had no interest in actually participating.

High on a hill—a location we tried three different times over the course of the week, and began calling "High Above Courtside"—a bull answered our calls loudly, and frequently. But he never stepped into view. Determined to be patient, we worked that area for three hours, until the setting sun forced us back to camp for the day.

Over the course of an enjoyable day, we had seen two moose (including one before sunrise), three grouse, two deer that frolicked in the shallows of Cassidy Deadwater, a rabbit, and two coyotes that seemed more interested in finding the source of our calls than the moose did. We ate like kings (and a queen), gobbling down sandwiches for lunch and pork loin for dinner.

But at the end of the day, it was a no-moose Monday. Just like I planned. Honest.

OK. Maybe terrible isn't the word proper word for our Tuesday. We did have fun. We did hear some interesting things. And we did have one cheap thrill, when a logger drove by and told us that a huge bull moose was wallowing in a bog, not a mile away from the spot we were hunting. But at the end of the day, we had nothing to show for our efforts but this—knowledge.

Not that there's anything wrong with that, of course. We tried everything we could think of, we went to a few new places and hunted more diligently than the day before. But before we talk more about that, it's important to talk about this: Alpo.

The highlight of an otherwise unremarkable day, I figure, was the Alpo. Breakfast in a moose camp (or deer camp or fishing camp) is always impressive. Put Chris Lander in charge of cooking it, and you will eat exceptionally well. Lander, you see, cooks up a mean skillet of Alpo.

Alpo, of course, is not really Alpo. It is, in fact, actually prepared with human consumption in mind. But the only time I eat it is when I hang out with the Landers and we're miles away from civilization.

"Alpo" is a Landerese word for corned beef hash. And all you really need to know is this—when it slides out of a can into a sizzling skillet, you'd swear it looks as though the morning menu features dog food. Trust me, it's far better than dog food, but just don't ask me (or my sister) how I know.

Breakfast was Alpo and eggs and sausage and bacon. We hunted through lunch and then for dinner we ate Pete Warner's patented pasta-in-a-pot, which we took to calling Petey Pasta. Picture lasagna, without the flat noodles, and add about three times the recommended meat and cheese, and you'll get a fairly accurate picture.

So, back to the hunt. As it turned out, the logger's tip didn't pan out. Mr. Moose had vacated the bog before we could get there. And the wind blew all day, making calling difficult. We even tried tuning Chris Lander's satellite radio to the all-Elvis channel to change our hunting karma. The first song we heard seemed appropriate—"That's All Right."

"That's all we needed was a little Elvis," Chris told me with a grin. As it turned out, the moose didn't care much for The King. It got so bad at one point that we began to go a bit bonkers. Warner, in fact, admitted that the hours of waiting for the faint call of a distant moose were taking their toll.

"I've been straining to listen so much that I'm starting to hear people laughing," he said. "And voices."

Later that day, I started to experience the same sensation. But the day wasn't a total loss as Warner did see an otter swimming in the Deadwater. And we did hear real moose making the sounds we'd been trying to replicate on the Phantom. The cow was urgent. The bull answered back. Every ten seconds or so, the cow would moan. And moan. And moan. The lesson for the day: We weren't calling nearly as aggressively as real moose do. And on Wednesday, we planned to change all that.

I did, after all, want to get a moose on Wednesday. Did I already mention that?

On the way out of camp on Wednesday morning, a few big deadlines loomed. First and foremost was the one placed upon us by Bridget Brown—if we didn't shoot a moose before 8 a.m., we wouldn't get photographic evidence of our expertise, or lack thereof. She had to get back to Bangor.

Kingsbury was heading out at lunchtime. Warner had to leave by Thursday morning. And by Friday, Chris and I each had to be back in Bangor. The clock was ticking. But we were ready, thanks to some secret weapons: Billy and Timmy Lander had been very, very busy boys. While we had been hunting for two days, the older Lander boys had been scouting. Periodically, we'd meet up and they'd tell us what they'd found.

On Tuesday, they had found two spots that were full of moose sign, with no evidence of having been hunted. We went to one early in the morning, then headed back to the bog the trucker had told us about.

Neither of those spots panned out. It was now 8 a.m. Bridget Brown headed to back to town. We were on our own. That's when things got really interesting. At the second spot scouted by the Landers boys, we parked at the end of a long, grassy skidder path and walked a half mile, just as they directed. We set up our call, hid behind some brush, and got to work. Encouraged by the tryst we'd overheard the night before, I began pushing buttons feverishly.

The cow was in heat, I reasoned. And the bull had to be interested. Every fifteen seconds or so, I hit another sequence of buttons. Estrous cow. Bull grunt. Bull grunt. Cow. Bull. Cow.

As I looked at the control panel, trying to decide on my next mating salvo, an urgent voice in my ear told me my efforts wouldn't be needed.

There he is, someone said. It could have been Kingsbury. It could have been Chris Lander. But when I looked up, I saw a modest bull moose, broadside, fifty yards away. Trying not to fumble, I handed

Kingsbury the call's remote control, unslung my rifle, lay it on my shooting stick, and took aim. One shot rang out. The moose dropped where he stood.

After two minutes, he regained his feet. Chris and I fired at the same time, and the bull fell for the last time. The entire episode happened quickly, I thought. Warner wasn't so sure. When the bull appeared, he wasn't holding the call. He had heard the crack of a twig. And he had been staring at the opening in the trees when the moose stepped out.

"I'll tell you what, buddy," Warner said. "Between the time we saw that moose come out and the time you shot him, it seemed like eight days."

It was 10:25, and the hunt was over. Just in time for our respective deadlines.

The old maxim of moose hunting holds that all the fun ends when you pull the trigger. In this case, that wasn't true. The bull fell four feet from the skidder path, and we were able to drive a truck right to it. From the time we pulled the trigger, it took us an hour and twelve minutes to field-dress the moose and load him into the truck. Yes, I was counting. (I did have a story to write, after all.) All the credit goes to the Lander boys, who are experts at the field-dressing process and took over the messy chore.

By 1:30 p.m., we had tagged the moose at Raymond's Country Store in Northeast Carry. By 2:30, we were eating heaping helpings of Billy Chili, Billy Lander's food offering. And by 6:30, we were eating again, feasting on the baby back ribs that Timmy Lander had brought. (I know, it sounds gluttonous, but we took a lot of food with us, and we decided to get rid of as much as we could.)

For the record, I'm not exactly sure how much the bull weighed. The scale initially said 636 pounds, but there was a lot of ice involved in that unofficial measurement. After removing all the ice I could reach (one bag was pesky, and I couldn't extract it from the moose), the scale read 589 pounds.

That's the weight I'll remember, and that's the story I'll tell . . . and tell . . . and tell.

The moose had an eight-point rack with a spread of just under thirty inches. Modest, to say the least, but we weren't complaining. In fact, as the sun set that night, all of us kept reliving the hunt. Each part of the week was fair game, and repeating our own tales to those who were there to witness it all didn't seem in the least bit redundant. In fact, it seemed necessary.

Eventually, we turned in and later we returned to town.

We learned. We laughed. We ate too much. And at the end of the day, a moose even decided to take part in our hunt on Wednesday.

Just like I'd hoped.

Honest.

38. The Epic Buck Contest

A couple years ago, David Wardwell sidled up at a rod and gun club function and began a conversation with the words outdoor writers love to hear.

"I might have a story for you one of these days," the Penobscot man said.

Over the next five minutes, Wardwell, known as "Cappy" to his friends, told me an as-yet-unfinished tale about family, friends, hunting and the fruitless pursuit of a truly big deer. Any truly big deer. The premise was simple: Bag a buck that weighs more than two hundred pounds, and win a prize.

Sounds simple . . . or maybe not.

When the Wardwell boys and a few friends began their quest at a hunting camp in Penobscot, Cappy explained, all were much younger men. Ronald Reagan had just been elected president, but hadn't begun serving his first term. The year was 1979. Cappy Wardwell was twenty-nine, and figured it wouldn't take too long for him or one of the other hunters to cash in. After all, he and his brothers, Toby and Peter ("Sneaky Pete" to those in camp), had learned plenty about hunting at the hand of their father, Millard, an accomplished hunter and trapper who shared his knowledge and passion for the outdoors.

"One night we started talking and nobody had ever killed a two hundred-pound deer," he said. "So we said, 'OK, let's everybody throw in five bucks.'"

Five bucks a year got you in the pool. Another five bucks and you'd be in for the yearly big buck contest—no two hundred-pounder was necessary.

A few years ago, with the number of hunters dwindling, Cappy and his brothers eliminated the yearly prize, and began putting ten dollars a year into the two hundred-pounder pool. As years went by, the Wardwells began seeing more and more gray hair in their beards, but still nobody won.

A few times, they came close. Cappy shot a one hundred and ninety-one-pounder several years back—his biggest deer ever. His brother, Peter, came even closer, with a buck that weighed one-hundred and ninety-eight pounds. If it had been two hundred on the nose, though, Cappy Wardwell said his brother wouldn't have cashed in the prize. The Wardwells wanted no doubt that the deer was a genuine two hundred-pounder. So the pile of money, stowed in a plastic license holder for the past twenty-seven years, kept growing.

Hunters grew older, some stopped coming to Maine to join in, and those who'd have liked to get in on the action were told they could, but only for a price. The group kept exacting records and knew precisely how much each of the charter member of the pool had paid in over the years. If you wanted to join late, you needed to pay the same amount of "dues" that they had since the beginning.

The location of their forays changed over the years. At first, the woods around Penobscot were the hunting grounds, but eventually they moved into the big north woods. For the last three years, the hunting party journeyed north of Chamberlain Lake with a large army tent and all the equipment needed for a week in the woods.

A week or so ago, an excited Cappy Wardwell called to tell me the good news.

"I just thought I'd give you a holler and tell you the big buck pool has come to an end," he said.

On November 6, the hunters awoke to three inches of fresh snow. A welcome sight, yes, but the presence of tracking snow didn't seem to improve their karma.

"We had four vehicles, drove the roads all day long and never cut a track all day long," Cappy Wardwell said. "We got back for supper and were very, very discouraged."

The next day—election day—was much, much better.

"We cut a big buck's track, and he was on the tail of a doe," Cappy Wardwell said. "Toby said, 'Do you think it's worth tracking?' I said, 'Oh, yeah.'"

Toby's deer camp name is "Tracker," reflecting his expertise on the trail of deer, so he was glad to hear the answer.

"We've got all day," Toby Wardwell said.

It didn't take that long. After a couple of hours on the trail, the Wardwells caught up with the doe.

"I stepped out of a skidder road and the doe was standing there, looking at me, about forty-five yards away," David Wardwell said. "We waited probably a good twelve to fifteen minutes. She couldn't wind us, but she decided something wasn't right. She spun, stepped off, and started blowing every time she hit the ground."

The Wardwells knew that the buck was likely nearby, so they waited for their chance. David carried the gun, a Thompson Contender single-shot rifle chambered in .375 Winchester. In the chamber was a special bullet he had asked his father to hand load for him about three years ago.

"I told him, 'Load this one up [for me]. I'm going to kill a 200-pound deer with it,'" Cappy Wardwell said.

Finally, after twenty-seven years of effort and countless miles of driving and trudging, Cappy got the chance he'd been waiting for.

"About thirty seconds [after the doe left] I see some movement," he said. "[Then] fifty, fifty-five yards, the old boy came out."

Cappy shot the deer with that single special bullet, watched as it bolted out of sight, then sat down to wait for a bit. On the videotape of the hunt that Cappy sent along with a few photos, his excitement was tangible as he and Toby moved forward to recover the deer.

"Oh, baby, light my fire," he bellowed, raising his arms above his head as he spied the deer, just thirty yards from where he'd shot it. Even on video, it's plainly apparent that the critter is a big deer, the deer of a lifetime, easily a two-hundred-pounder with a massive thirteen-point rack.

Later that night, they got ready to hoist the buck onto a special game pole to weigh it for the first time. Wherever these hunters, go, Cappy Wardwell explains, this game pole goes with them. It's more than a hunk of cedar, you see. It's the tree that provided the cedar boughs that another hunting buddy, Bobby Hileman, was laid to rest upon two years ago. When Hileman died, Toby Wardwell built the casket, and Hileman's widow wanted to lay her husband to rest on a bed of cedar. The three Wardwell boys headed to Pete Wardwell's land and cut that tree, now known in camp as "Bobby's Big Buck Pole."

"Where we go, it goes," Cappy Wardwell wrote. "So Bobby's always at camp with us."

As the buck was lifted onto Bobby's Big Buck Pole, it quickly became apparent the pool was closed. But by how much?

Plenty.

The burly thirteen-pointer weighed 258 pounds, field-dressed, and without the heart and liver. After that, of course, there was the small matter of the prize money—twenty-seven years of big buck dues, payable to Cappy Wardwell.

The grand total was $1,075.

Cappy said there were no hard feelings in camp. All of the hunters—Toby and Pete Wardwell, Larry Hall and Richard Lord—were excited.

"It's just like every one of them shot the deer," Cappy Wardwell said. "It was the best week of camp we've ever had. It didn't matter who put him on the ground."

All of which begs the question: What do you do now? Is there another Big Buck pool in the offing?

"No sir. Never. I'm never, ever going to get into a two hundred-pound pool again," Cappy Wardwell said with a chuckle. "Like my brother Peter said when that deer hit the ground, 'The curse is over.' It's just like the Boston Red Sox. "It's like that darned pool was a jinx on us."

Without the added pressure of that pool, Cappy figures he and his brothers can now enjoy just hunting. Cappy has been hunting for forty-four years now. Pete has put in forty-three autumns. And Toby has forty-two years of hunting to his credit.

"Now we can go out and hunt deer, and not have to worry about that darned pool any more," Cappy said.

39. Hunting Lessons

Ever since I joined the blaze-orange brigade and began spending hours perched in trees, skulking through the woods and sitting on stumps, I have insisted on treating my November obsession as a learning experience. That, for the uninitiated, is a pretty nifty way for deerless deer hunters to rationalize the fact that we're spending hours sitting in trees and on stumps and looking for piles of deer excrement.

Having another "learning experience," after all, sounds a lot more fun than "wasting another afternoon sitting by myself in the woods."

Last week, I took a week of vacation, spent most of it in the woods, and I learned a few more things I'd like to share. I never shot a deer. Never saw a deer. But learn? You bet I did.

Lesson No. 1: Woodpeckers travel in packs. Honest. At least those in Otis do. I'm not a bird expert and can't quite figure out which variety of woodpecker I've been watching, but I have learned that on certain days (usually the days that seem perfect for deer hunting) these tough-billed, redheaded noisemakers descend, en masse. On two different days, I watched as eight or ten of the birds surrounded my tree stand and began pecking. Some pecked live trees. Some pecked fallen trees. Some (apparently the not-too-bright woodpeckers) pecked leaf-covered rocks.

At first, I thought it was cute. Then I thought it was cool. Eventually, I recognized it for what it was—a concerted effort by the denizens of the woods to cover for each other. With all the racket, I couldn't possibly hear any approaching deer. And approach they did. I didn't see them, of course. But I'm certain that they tip-toed past me while their beaked buddies provided the cover noise.

Lesson No. 2: In the woods, there is no such thing as a shortcut. I learned this valuable lesson (again) after deciding to abandon my swamp and meet up with a hunting buddy at his car. Spying a ridge that I had scoured for deer droppings on more than one occasion (several years earlier, unfortunately), I set my course and started tromping on what I was sure was a shorter route to the road. A path awaited. At least, a path awaited the last time I trudged to the top of the ridge. What could have changed in a few years? How about this: Everything.

Apparently, a pack of woodpeckers had laid siege to the area, knocked down all the trees and created a mess of blow-downs. Of course, it was impossible to appreciate the magnitude of the mess until I was in the middle of it. And by that point, I figured I had no choice but to keep clambering over toppled woodpecker debris. It was, after all, a shortcut. And I was determined to prove that my uncanny sense of direction was accurate.

It was, I think. But I also think that the woodpeckers destroyed the path I was looking for all in a premeditated attempt to get me lost. Or something like that.

Lesson No. 3: After a day of hunting, after everyone else in camp leaves you alone as they run into town on various errands, be very careful about your recreational choices. What a day it had been! I had tromped in the woods, had a wonderful time and seen plenty of evidence of deer (and woodpeckers). With camp to myself, I realized that the old wood stove was really cranking, and I decided to vent a bit of hot air by propping the door open. Then, I headed for the most comfortable chair, which coincidentally sits underneath the brightest gaslight, and cracked open my new book.

Good idea, in theory. Bad idea, in practice. The book was *20th Century Ghosts*. It was written by a young guy named Joe Hill. You might have heard of his dad, who has also sold a few books over the years. His name is Stephen King.

For the record, his son, Joe, is good at sharing scary tales. Very good. As it turns out, too good. At first, I was fine. Then I turned a page. Got to a pretty creepy part. And outside (with the door propped wide open, mind you) the noises started. Low at first. Moaning. Then high-pitched and yipping. Then screaming and howling. Right on cue, the coyotes had come for dinner.

And I was on the menu, or so it seemed in my mind. I crept to the door, shut it tightly, and hunkered down in the well-lit hunting camp.

After years of reading the master of horror, that's one lesson I didn't have to head into the woods to learn.

40. Calling a Turkey. Or a Crow?

Against all odds, and despite a couple of unpredictably predictable miscues, Hunting Buddy and I had quite a time May 3, the opening day of the state's wild turkey hunting season. We saw birds. We talked to birds. We watched birds vanish into the woods. And eventually, we found one that agreed to come home to dinner.

But I'm getting ahead of myself. This is, after all, a hunting story. As such, getting there is more than half the fun. Even if you eventually end up knee-deep in turkey feathers. Even if you end up thinking your neighbors think you're crazy. Even if.

So, let's start at the beginning. Not the waking up (everyone has to wake up early to turkey hunt, after all). And not when the owl hooted in the pre-dawn gloom (although that was pretty cool, too). No, let's move forward an hour or two, to the point at which both Hunting Buddy and I had begun wondering if we weren't in for yet another of those days.

You know those days, I bet. The animals don't show up. You sit on the cold ground and swat black flies. You hear the distant reports of shotguns and convince yourself that some hunter a couple miles away just stole the bird that, eventually, would have wandered into range of your own shotgun.

And then, one of those days turned into something else entirely. The lowdown turkey thieves had not actually stolen our bird. In fact, our bird, or birds, as it turned out, were right behind us. And they wanted to talk. Man, did they want to talk.

Unfortunately, they did not want to court our very attractive hen turkey decoy. And unfortunately, they did not want to venture within shotgun range. But they talked. And talked. And talked. Right up until they decided my efforts with a mouth call left something to be desired.

But I was lucky. I was prepared. I moved on to Plan B: The foolproof (or so they say) electronic calling system. By pushing a button, I could yelp like a girl. I could gobble like a boy. I could scratch for

John Holyoke practicing a moose call. Photo by Bridget Brown, Bangor Daily News.

food. I could flap my turkey wings and fly to the ground. And I could crow like, well, like a crow. Remember that last part.

These calls are manufactured locally and are impressive. Plug in interchangeable computer chips, and your call can talk turkey or deer or moose or coyote. Which would have been really cool if I had replaced my batteries after deer season last fall. Hmm.

So, after a couple of hours into our morning, Hunting Buddy and I sat in the forest, staring at a not-too-distant loudspeaker suffering a case of battery-induced laryngitis. Being Hunting Buddy's self-appointed mentor (and being eager to blame something on someone else), I made an executive decision.

"Sneak up there and bring that speaker back," I whispered. "And don't scare off the turkeys."

After switching out the batteries and laying the speaker at my feet, I leaned back against my tree, smiled, and pushed a button. My speaker yelped, just like a girl turkey. And in the distance, the boy turkeys gobbled their approval. At this point, I'd love to tell you that through superb calling and amazing patience and skill, Hunting Buddy and I were able to talk those birds into walking back into view.

I'd like to tell you that we fired two perfectly synchronized shots, and that each of us bagged a bird, and that we staged a seven-course, two-turkey barbecue feast that our neighbors are still raving about. Unfortunately, I can't. Those birds never returned. They just stood out there, somewhere, and gobbled. Deep down, I know they were making fun of us.

Fortunately, another bird had other ideas. For about ten minutes, we worked the new arrival. We yelped softly. He gobbled and walked closer. Then he worked his way around us, always just outside of range. Then he stepped close enough, but ended up behind a blowdown. And then, I did a very bad thing.

Ever so slowly, I reached for the remote control to the (theoretically) foolproof electronic call. Slowly, I felt with my gloved hand for the proper button, the one that would issue a soft, plaintive, seductive "yelp." This yelp would urge the bird onward. Toward us. Toward the tagging station. Toward my table. I pushed the button. The wrong button.

And my foolproof call did exactly what I asked of it—it blasted the digital voice of a crow. The turkey, as you might imagine, was not impressed. Neither was I. Hunting Buddy, however, thought it was hilarious.

Eventually, after Hunting Buddy stopped laughing, I found the right button. Eventually, I yelped. And eventually, the turkey hopped up onto the blowdown, stood proudly, and volunteered for dinner duty. All of which explains why, last Monday afternoon, I ended up in my backyard, which I had transformed into, well, let's call it a turkey preparation area.

Which, if you were standing in my neighbor's backyard last Monday, explains why you might have looked up and seen me standing there, knee-deep in feathers, with every knife I own lined up neatly on a table. It explains the large, dead bird on that table and the hastily printed Internet instructions on field dressing and skinning a turkey held down by paper weights that looked a lot like knives.

And it explains the bush-loppers. OK. Maybe it doesn't explain the bush-loppers. But it does explain the marinated turkey breasts you may have smelled when I grilled them Tuesday evening. And it certainly explains why I've been smiling ever since.

I do love it when a plan comes together, you see. Or something like that.

41. Katie

For as long as he can remember, Jay Robinson of Woodville has owned dogs. Bird dogs, actually. English pointers, specifically. And for years, come October, Robinson has taken those dogs afield. Mary and Button. Susan and Mike. Sadie and Diamond. And then there was Katie.

Katie didn't start off as Jay Robinson's dog. Instead, the dog was a faithful hunting companion of Wilmot "Wiggie" Robinson, Jay's dad. Wiggie, a popular Maine guide, died in 2007. Many of the state's outdoorsmen mourned. Katie moved in with Jay shortly thereafter.

Over the subsequent three autumns, Katie joined Jay Robinson's rotation of bird dogs. Last fall, she split time in the coverts with Diamond. Katie was aging, thirteen years years old, now—and trotted with a shambling, lopsided gait. The younger Diamond did the bulk of the work, but every other day or so, Jay, also a guide, would hook

Collars of bird dogs that Jay Robinson has owned sit in a position of honor in his Woodville home. Photo by John Holyoke.

a bell around the old girl's neck, set her loose and follow as Katie did what she'd been bred to do—hunt.

Then, on a cold February morning, Jay Robinson lost his dog.

"I usually go out, mid-morning," Robinson explained. "I let 'em out [of their heated kennel] and they just run around in the yard."

While the dogs run and play and do their business, Robinson cleans up the messes that tend to pile up when dogs are left to do what dogs do.

"I come around the corner, and they're usually on the porch, waiting for me, wagging their tails so they can go in and eat," Robinson said. "[This day], I come around the corner and Katie's not there."

Robinson said he didn't worry about Katie's absence at first. She was a curious dog, after all. And he was sure she just headed into the woods to check out a few new smells.

"I didn't think too much of it at the time, because Katie's always chasing squirrels," he said. "But she always comes right back. I have to do a little calling, but she'll come right back."

Not this time.

"I kept hollering and hollering. I got the bell out and blew a whistle," Robinson said. "I went up and down the road. All the time I'm getting more and more worried about her. She might have got hit by a car."

Time passed. Katie remained missing. And gradually, Jay Robinson gave up hope.

"Days go by, and days turn into weeks, and I thought, well, the dog must be dead," Robinson said. "That was too bad. She was a really good dog, and I've had her a few years, and she was dad's dog. I'd always hunted over her. I [was going to] miss her."

As the weeks passed, Robinson moved on. He began working with his other two dogs, Diamond and Abby. He watched as winter turned to spring.

"That's the end of the story," he thought. "And I always wondered what happened to my dog."

About two weeks ago, in true rural Maine fashion, Robinson found out. Robinson said he was in his front yard, cutting up a deer that a motorist had hit and killed the night before.

"I ran right out there in my slippers. It was a Massachusetts guy. A young guy. I asked him, 'Do you want that deer?'" Robinson said.

The answer was "No."

And that was fine with Robinson, who called a game warden to get permission to keep the deer, then hung the carcass in a tree overnight. The next morning, he got down to some down-home butchering.

"This vehicle pulls up along the side of the road and pulls into my dooryard," Robinson said.

Robinson thought the driver might be looking to score some free venison, or to talk to him about how he came to have a deer hanging from his tree. That wasn't the case at all.

"I walked over and said, 'What can I do for you?'" Robinson said. "I looked in the front seat beside him and there sits Katie. I couldn't believe it."

The stranger told Robinson that back in February, he went to his front door one morning —the morning after Robinson had lost track of Katie—and met a new friend.

"There was a dog, a friendly dog, wagging her tail like she knew where she needed to be," Robinson said. "I could just picture her, jogging up the road, two miles away."

Robinson said the stranger, he still isn't sure of the man's name, wasn't sure how the dog had come to be on his front porch.

"He took her in. He wondered whose dog it was. She had a collar, but no nametag," Robinson said. "He thought, well, nobody owns this dog, or maybe they didn't want her and dropped her off."

The man took the dog to the vet, fed her and treated her well, Robinson said. Then, a couple months later, he learned that a Woodville man had lost a similar dog in February.

"He'd checked around and nobody knew [who owned Katie]," Robinson said. "Then he went to Lennie's [Superette] one day for gas and groceries. He saw another fellow [who said] 'I know a guy who has English pointers, too, and he lost a dog a few months back. He's looking for a dog and this might be his dog.' The guy said, 'It might be. I found this dog a few months back.'"

That, you might think, is where this story ends. In fact, that's where Jay Robinson thought it was going to end.

"I thought, 'This is great. I've got Katie back, and everybody will live happily ever after,'" Robinson said.

Then Robinson talked to the man who'd found his dog, learned a bit more, and made a decision that changed everything.

"I thought I should repay the guy for all the dog food and for taking her to the vet," Robinson said. "All the time he's saying, 'I really like this dog. Really good dog.'

"Then he said, 'I've got cancer. I might not live another year,'" Robinson said. "I thought about it for a few seconds and decided, this man should own my dog. He's had her for a few months and got really attached to her."

Robinson is adamant in his belief that he did nothing out of the ordinary. At first, he was uncomfortable telling his story to even family members. When he did, and they encouraged him to let his friends on Facebook know about finding Katie, he realized how powerful the story could be. But he realized that he didn't necessarily want the praise that he was sure to receive.

"I want to stress, I'm no saint. It's no big deal," he said. "Maybe somebody in the same situation would do the same thing."

Robinson did admit, however, that he's thought about how his father would have felt about him giving Katie to a stranger who'd looked after her during a cold Maine winter. It had been his dog, after all.

"I think maybe he'd want me to do the same thing," Robinson said. "Maybe in the same situation he would have done the same thing. And I'm thinking, this is a good thing."

So, now Katie has a new owner. But come autumn, if she's up to it, old Katie might find that she has more than one master to please.

The new owner made a deal with Robinson, you see. First, Robinson is welcome to visit Katie any time he wants.

And second, when the leaves start turning, and when the woodcock and grouse start flying, always a favorite time of year for the Robinson men, Jay said he'll likely spend a bit more time with his old dog.

"[The new owner said] 'You can take the dog hunting, if you want, come October,'" Robinson said.

42. Taunted by a Red Squirrel

When opening day of deer season rolls around, my hunting buddies and I are no different from many others. We are traditionalists. While that word may mean different things to different people, to us it means something pretty simple. We go back to the cozy stand of woods that we hunt every opening day, or at least every opening day when youth hockey games or work or other facets of real life don't require our attention, and we hunt.

I sit. Billy and Chris walk. They see signs of deer. I see signs of leaves falling off trees. And signs of squirrels. And, if I'm lucky, signs of woodpeckers. Then, hours later, we meet up, talk about all the things we saw (or didn't see) and go our separate ways.

In the seven years we've hunted together, this has been our tradition. So has this—no deer has ever participated in our opening day festivities. Tradition is great, isn't it? But every tradition can use a bit of a boost now and then, and this year we arrived at the appointed place (Otis) at the appointed time (way too early) determined to forge a new, more productive tradition.

Red squirrel taunts John Holyoke. Photo by John Holyoke.

A more deer-inclusive tradition, you might say. At least that was the plan. This year's deer-season opener presented an enjoyable change of pace for our hunting party because the weather was finally crisp and November-ish, rather than balmy and September-ish, as in some previous years.

How crisp it would be (or how long I'd decide to sit in my chilly tree), I couldn't really tell. Therefore, it was essential to do everything I could to remain comfortable. Not that I'm a wimp, mind you. It's just that I've learned that it's hard to sit still when you're shivering and your teeth are chattering. Hunters brighter than me have told me that sitting still is important.

Therefore, I brought out the secret weapon. Not to shoot. To sit on. When I received this secret weapon as a gift a couple years back, I immediately chuckled, thinking there'd never, ever be a situation when a hardy Maine hunter like me would resort to such a device. The first time the mercury dropped below thirty, however, I carefully read the attached instructions and followed them to the letter.

I took the gel pack out of the seat cushion.

I tossed it in the microwave.

I nuked it for five minutes.

Then I quickly tucked it into my pack before anyone saw it and made fun of me. Yes, I own a microwaveable hunting seat. And I use it. OK. Maybe I am a wimp. But on Saturday, as the wind blew and the deer ignored me and I sat in my cold tree stand, I was a warm-rumped wimp. And there's something to be said for that.

While deer don't participate in my hunts very often, other critters do. In fact, you could say it's a bit of a tradition. In China, last year was the Year of the Pig. In Otis, it was the Year of the Woodpecker.

Each day I was on the stand, a few would fly through and provide a bit of percussive entertainment for me.

Every other year I've hunted those woods has been the Year of the Red Squirrel. This year, apparently, is no different. As I sat on my toasty-warm seat Saturday morning, it didn't take long for my old pal Red to show up. At first, there were footsteps in the woods. Years ago, I would have assumed those cracking branches were caused by a deer.

Now, I'm a real hunter. I know better. And from the moment I sat down I knew it would be just a matter of time before Red stopped by to taunt me. It didn't take long.

My second indication that I had a visitor was the sound of tiny claws clambering up my tree. A few minutes later, after he'd found a nice perch far above my stand, the little beast began his barrage. Bark fell on my head. Then twigs. Then more bark. Red was here. And he was mad. Bark-throwing, twig-tossing mad. A while later, he scurried across a branch and made a perfect dismount to the forest floor.

A half an hour later, he was back to reiterate his message. This time, he was loud . . . and mad. I heard the whisper of tiny footfalls on the tree. My tree. Or, perhaps more accurately, *his* tree. Then, as I peered to the side, looking for (nonexistent) deer, I caught a flash of movement just above my head. Red was four feet above me, a couple feet higher than I could reach, staring me in the eye.

I glared. He glared back.

Then he began to scream in my face like . . . well … like an angry squirrel. Not long after that, Red called it quits and climbed out of the tree. Soon enough, so did I. Real life beckoned. I had things to do, and places to go. As I trudged back to my truck, I heard a red squirrel. He wasn't chattering. He wasn't screaming.

This time, I swear he was laughing.

All of which made Saturday just another traditional opening day in my favorite deer woods.

43. A Lovesick Moose

In order to participate in Maine's annual moose hunt, you, or one of your friends, has to be lucky. Hunting permits are earned by random lottery, and only the winners and their designated sub-permittees are allowed to take part in the event.

If you're not lucky, however, there are other options. At least that's what Chris Lander explained it to me during the summer, when he hatched a plan for another kind of outdoor adventure. We have collaborated on two moose hunts in the last five years, but this year, no one in our hunting party bagged a permit. Still, Lander wanted to go moose hunting, or something like that.

"We should go up into the woods during the week between moose seasons," he told me. "We can still call moose. I'd like to get some good video and photos."

Thus, the first Catch-and-Release Moose Hunt for the Unlucky began to take shape. We quickly got my co-worker Pete Warner on board for the festivities. Warner is a fun guy to hang around with and has a habit of doing things to spice up a trip (much to his own chagrin). Like the time he stepped in an ice hole while fishing. Or the time he dropped a full plate of chili and hot dogs on the floor at moose camp. Or the time, well, you get the point.

Eventually, we decided that adding two days of bird hunting to our Sunday of moose-peeping made sense. Eventually, we decided to scrap the part of the plan that called for us roughing it in an Army

Pete Warner. Photo by John Holyoke.

tent in the North Maine Woods, opting instead to stay at a Brassua Lake camp owned by Lander's father-in-law and his brothers.

And eventually, we ended up getting accosted by a lovesick moose in aptly named Misery Township.

Well, "accosted" might not be the right word. "Pursued" works better. So does "stalked." Whichever word you choose, one thing's certain—the moose liked me more than I liked him.

But I'm getting ahead of myself.

First, it's important to realize that the bird hunting would have been fantastic but for a few small complications. For example, the best action we saw for ruffed grouse came on Sunday. We had designated Sunday as our moose-peeping day. And it turns out that the state frowns upon bird hunting on Sundays. Knowing that, we left the shotguns at camp, took our moose calls into the woods—and saw plenty of birds.

Everywhere we drove, we saw grouse. They were in the roads. They were on the side of the roads. They flushed and flew into nearby thickets. In the spirit of Red Sox fans everywhere, our rally cry became "Wait until tomorrow." Come tomorrow, we knew that we'd each fill our four-bird bag limit. We'd feast on grouse. And then we'd do the same thing the next day. No doubt about it.

The moose, however, were a bit shy. We found likely places and made moose-like noises. We grunted like bulls. We moaned like cows. And no moose joined in. Just before sunset, our efforts paid off. Not that our calling had anything to do with our success, mind you. It was, I guess, a simple matter of three unlucky prospective moose hunters having a bit of dumb luck.

Two moose stood in a clearing. A small bull and cow grazed, and paid little mind to Lander as he leaned out of the truck window and got the video footage he had wanted. Warner and I crept back and forth and snapped photos of the feeding pair.

It was, we all said, very cool. It was just what we'd hoped for. And the next day, we'd have even better luck on the birds. Or not.

Truck spotting. Photo by John Holyoke.

Monday dawned cloudy, and we headed back out and back into places with names like Taunton and Raynham Academy Grant and Sapling Township and, of course, Misery. We covered mile after mile on the roads in vain. The birds had vanished. Well, all except one foolish grouse that allowed me to take a remarkably easy shot. Which I missed.

Riding roads wasn't working out. A change in tactics was needed. So we switched to a country music station on Lander's Sirius satellite radio. Then we tried comedy. Then we tried classic rock. Nothing improved our karma. Finally, we hopped out of the truck at a likely looking spot and acted like bird dogs, taking turns walking through the woods in hopes of flushing a lurking grouse.

That's when things got interesting. Not that we flushed any lurking grouse, mind you. Instead, we learned that a 250-pound man waddling

167

Earle Hannigan looks at old photos after a day afield near Brassua Lake. Photo by John Holyoke.

noisily through the woods sounds nothing like a bird dog. He does, however, sound a lot like a clumsy cow moose in need of a boyfriend.

At least that's our explanation for the Misery Moose Episode. I was the bird dog at the time, walking through the alders and birches in search of grouse. Lander and Warner walked the road, waiting for me to flush a bird and provide them a shot they never got. After two hundred yards of bird-dogging, I popped back out of the woods.

And just behind Lander and Warner, in the middle of the road, was a young bull moose. This moose wasn't just standing. He wasn't just watching. He was walking toward us. With a purpose. With (or so we decided) love on his mind.

"How close do we let him get?" someone asked.

"Not much closer," someone answered.

"How do we get him to stop?" someone else asked.

Before my hunting partners decided to offer me up as a sacrifice, I told the moose . . . well . . . I told him I didn't like him in that way. That's what I was trying to say, anyway.

What came out of my mouth may have been, "Hey! Arrrrrrr!"

Whatever I said, it worked. The moose got no closer than thirty yards. Warner got some photos. But Lander had left his video camera in the truck, and missed out on the opportunity. At my urging, we left Misery before Lander retrieved the camera and decided it would make perfect sense to send me back into the woods to try to re-create the moment.

For two days, we drove those roads. For two days, the birds refused to participate in bird season. But on Monday night, as twilight approached (and as we gave up on our futile efforts to bag a bird), we stopped by a spot where we'd seen the hind end of a retreating moose the night before.

"Want to set up and call for a bit?" Lander asked. "Maybe we'll get lucky."

We set up. And we got lucky. After just a couple of grunts, a moose responded. After a couple of cow imitations on the electronic call, the bushes were shaking. A big moose was coming.

Two minutes later, a burly bull stood just thirty-five yards away. His antlers were massive. He was massive. And thankfully, he didn't seem to think I was his long-lost cow.

Lander got his video. Warner got a few photos.

And I got away safely, without having to marry a moose.

All in all, it was a pretty lucky day. Just as we'd planned.

44. Please Come Back Mr. Squirrel

Not many years ago, I wrote a column in which I lamented the treatment I received in the Maine woods. Don't get me wrong, my fellow deer hunters were treating me fine. And even though no deer were participating in my (supposed) deer hunt, I was OK with that.

It was those darned red squirrels that were driving me nuts. They scurried to-and-fro, sounding exactly like a deer. More accurately, I suppose, they sounded exactly like what I assumed a deer would sound like if a deer ever walked close enough for me to hear them.

If that wasn't enough, the squirrels also served as an early warning system for all the alleged deer in the woods, climbing high in their trees and telling those deer exactly which tree the lazy hunter (me) was sitting in. At least, that's what I think they were doing. I had a hard enough time with Spanish and never took Squirrel 101, so I'll admit that I'm guessing.

The icing on the cake, you may recall, was when my little red nemesis climbed up my tree, perched four feet over my head and began pelting me with bark. Last year, when the squirrel (or a dead-ringer for the bark-chucker) showed up, I got serious. I got mean. I evicted the little loudmouth.

Rest assured, I did not harm the squirrel in question. I did not touch him (mostly because I was afraid he'd bite me, and I didn't want to have to explain a festering squirrel bite to a doctor, and I certainly didn't want my editors to make me write about it). But I got him. Man, did I get him.

I found that squirrels apparently are not fond of portly, middle-aged, tree-bound hunters who make mean, nasty faces at them. I bared my teeth and mouthed silent snarls (wouldn't want to have scared away all those deer, mind you), and after a few minutes of that, the squirrel got scared and ran away.

At least, I think he got scared. He might have thought I'd totally lost it, and may have decided that he'd rather not socialize with such a maladjusted heathen. But either way, he ran away. And he never came back.

For awhile, I thought that was a good thing. Today, as deer season reaches its halfway point, I realize that I was wrong. You hear that, Mr. Squirrel? I was wrong.

Over the past couple of years (since I acted so rudely, Mr. Squirrel), I've found that the woods are not the same. Well, let me rephrase that. The woods are exactly the same when it comes to the number of deer I see (zero). But a few years ago (when you still were around, Mr. Squirrel), I could count on at least a few thoroughly exhilarating false alarms every single time I went into the woods. Remember? You'd sneak around, doing your best deer tromp. I'd perk up and get ready to finally fill my deer tag.

Then, after a few tense minutes, you'd pop out from behind a tree and laugh. Man, you'd laugh. Later that day, you'd do the same thing. And the next day. And the day after that. Now, things are, well, boring.

I still sit in my tree stand. I still wait for deer. And still, nothing happens. Nothing. One day, I decided to spice things up. Get this, Mr. Squirrel. You'll love this.

I ate a granola bar. I know, eating a granola bar doesn't rate very high on the spice-it-up scale, but that ought to show you how boring things have been. As a matter of fact, eating that granola bar was the high point of hunting season so far. So, if you're out there, Mr. Squirrel, I've just got something to say.

I'm sorry. I miscalculated. If you come back, I won't make mean faces at you. I won't try to scare you off. I won't complain when you do your deer imitation.

In fact, if you come back, I might even offer you a piece of my next granola bar.

Family Matters

Finally, the most important section of this book. I won't overburden you by commenting too much—I think these essays speak for themselves. But here's a short explanation—the bonds of family are strong, and I've had the chance to share some poignant stories about other people's families over the years. And I've also been pretty open about my own family. Both are represented here. Thanks for reading.

45. Returning to Allagash

Late each summer, Mike Jarvis packs up his truck, sets a course from Brattleboro along the southern Vermont border to Allagash at the northern tip of Maine—a place he has come to love. But nobody would blame Jarvis if he didn't come back. Everybody would understand and forgive him. Still, every bear season (and again during deer season) Jarvis returns to his second family, to his second home, to the place his mother died, to memories that he and his father are still struggling to handle.

His mother, Nancy Jarvis, wasn't your typical woman. That becomes clear as her son talks about her, sharing many memories in the present tense, even nearly a decade after her death.

Look at Mike Jarvis and you see a small, sinewy, rugged outdoorsman who could (and will) track a deer for miles. He loves the woods. He loves to hunt. And he loves being in Allagash. Just like his mother did.

"She gets back three or four miles and doesn't worry about coming out," Jarvis says in the present tense, as if his mother were sitting beside us. "She knows her way in the woods and always comes out like she was supposed to."

Except for one time. There was nothing anyone could do for Nancy Jarvis on that day. Not Mike, who was back home in Brattleboro. Not Mike's dad, Phil, who was deer hunting with her. No one.

"I don't know if she was going into the [tree] stand or coming out of the stand," Mike Jarvis says, shaking his head slowly, speaking softly. "She had a massive heart attack."

When Nancy fell, her husband was there.

"For some reason, he had left his stand and gone to check on her," Mike Jarvis says. "Dad caught her when she was falling out of the tree."

Phil hiked two and a half miles out of the woods to get help, but nothing could be done. Just like that, Phil's wife and Mike's mom, one of the finest outdoorswomen you'd ever find, was gone.

"Them two were inseparable," Mike Jarvis says about his parents. "Anything one was doing, the other one was doing."

Yes, people would forgive Mike Jarvis if he didn't return to Allagash. Everybody would understand. But it hasn't worked out that way.

Late every summer, bear season arrives in these remote Maine woods. Small towns like Allagash bustle. Excitement is in the air. Old friendships are renewed, and new ones forged around a common interest. Also late every summer, Mike Jarvis returns to one such hunting town on the fringe of the massive north woods. This year he's actually a week early. His wife is pregnant. She's due on September 25, but she has a habit of delivering early.

"So I had to come up the first week, and I'm probably still pushing it," he says.

But he's here. Make no mistake about that. And Nancy Jarvis would surely be proud.

Phil and Nancy Jarvis headed to Allagash for the first time nearly twenty years ago. The family had always hunted near Moosehead Lake but had heard tales of big north woods bucks. They visited Allagash, looking for some land to buy, and stopped at a small restaurant called Two Rivers Lunch. That's where they met Tylor and Leitha Kelly, the owners. And that's when Mike Jarvis got his second family.

"They're good-hearted people and you can tell from your first impression of them that they're true to the heart," Mike Jarvis says. "And you know people like that when you see them and deal with them."

Soon, Mike was parking his camper on Kelly land when he came to hunt, even though his mom and dad had bought a parcel of land from the Kellys. Soon enough, Mike was sleeping in a spare room at Leitha and Tylor's house during bear season. Now, he helps guide Wade Kelly, Leitha and Tylor's son, put out bear baits and pitches in on a variety of other camp chores.

Among the twenty-two hunters in camp this week, there are many who know the Kellys well. Most veterans become increasingly involved in the camp's everyday chores. Jarvis, for one, has become more "guide" than "sport" over the years.

"We're pretty much family," Mike Jarvis said. "That's how I think of them and I'm sure that's how they look at me."

With one of the pillars of his life missing, Mike found comfort in another. The Kelly men were woodsmen like he and his dad. Leitha

Kelly is an accomplished hunter, just like his mom. Allagash felt right. It felt comfortable. It felt like a place he ought to be.

"That's why I come back," he says.

Mike Jarvis misses his mother, but finds solace in the woods he walks every time he returns to the place she loved so much, and every time he visits the family with which the Jarvises had become such good friends.

He doesn't forget what happened here. He hasn't entirely coped with it. But he has put his mother's death in context.

"If I had to go, I couldn't think of a better way to go, myself," he says.

Phil Jarvis has returned as well, at his son's coaxing. Last year, he and Mike hunted in Allagash for a couple of weeks. This year, Mike is hoping he can lure his father north for an even longer stay.

There is pain for both in visits like this, but there is peace to be found as well. One step at a time . . . One visit at a time . . . One year at a time.

Yes, as much as they like having him around camp, everybody would forgive Mike Jarvis if he didn't come back to Allagash. And everybody would understand. But Mike Jarvis is here. And he'll be back. Jarvis loves it here, you see. And he's still got important things he's got to do, eventually.

"I still haven't been back to the stand where she died," he says, quietly. "I still have to do that, someday. I'm not ready yet."

46. Tragedy and Grace

It was, to be sure, any mother's worst nightmare—a vibrant eighteen-year-old girl shot and killed in her own backyard. If any mother has the right to grieve, to mourn—even to hate—it is Jeri Brown. She will never see her daughter, Megan Ripley, again.

She will not watch the young equestrienne put her horse through its paces, nor watch Megan share her enthusiasm for the sport with curious children. She will not watch her marry or have children. A hunter's bullet, wardens say, made certain of that.

During a season when many of us take a moment to pause and think about things we can do to make a difference, Jeri Brown has done the unthinkable. She has asked us to pray.

Not for her daughter, but for the man who game wardens say shot and killed her. Take a moment to digest that. Now ask yourself if you could find the fortitude, the grace, the faith to do the same thing.

Most of us probably wouldn't. Jeri Brown is not most of us.

A week ago, Brown logged onto mainehorse.com, a website that her daughter enjoyed. She responded to the concerned equestrian community with a poignant message:

"Many have asked what they could do to help us out and I have a request for you . . . please keep Tim Bean and his family in your prayers," Brown wrote. "I dare say they are having a much harder time with all of this than we are. I cannot even begin to imagine how this man must feel. God had a plan and we are all a part of it.

"We trust and have the hope that Tim will heal and eventually put this behind him. Megan knew and loved one of his nieces. She let her ride Diva a few times and always answered the young girl's questions with patience and understanding. Megan had a heart for his niece and always told me what a nice girl she was. I hope she is doing okay through this."

So, if it were you, would you feel the same way? Could you?

On Wednesday, I made every journalist's least favorite telephone call. I called a grieving mother. I called Jeri Brown in South Paris. Understandably, she didn't want to talk. I didn't cajole, nor lobby for a minute of her time. I simply thanked the man on the other end of the telephone line, apologized for intruding, and hung up.

The questions, I suppose, remain.

What kind of inner strength does it take to ask people to pray for a man who is charged with causing you such pain and taking the life of someone you loved?

Or to take it a step further, how do I find that strength in myself? Does it even exist?

Jeri Brown and her family have been through an unthinkable tragedy. And they have responded with an incomprehensible grace of which all of us should take note. With Christmas approaching, Brown has provided us with a seasonal message much more tangible than those we usually find ourselves bombarded with.

Peace on earth. Good will toward men.

47. Goodbye, Pudge.

The house doesn't sound the same anymore. It doesn't feel the same, either.

Gone are the high-pitched sound of toenails on the kitchen hardwood—we called them "tippy-tappies"—that told my wife and I that our four-legged son was up to no good; scavenging for snacks we hadn't intended to leave within reach. Silenced are the midnight whimpers, accompanied by a barely audible sleep-bark that meant he was dreaming (about what, we always wondered) again. No longer do we drive into the yard and see his handsome square head peek over the windowsill, eager to welcome his masters home.

"I wish I could see a head in the window again," ten-year-old Georgia told us last night, as yet another return home went unwelcomed.

"So do I," I softly told her. Then, softer still: "So do I."

Pudge—Holyoke's Domino Pudge, according to his official American Kennel Club registry—died on March 25. He was in my arms, his head draped across my thighs, as I sat with him. He went as he had lived—peacefully.

Pudge was no stranger to *Bangor Daily News* readers. I wrote about him regularly—usually when he pulled one of his fast ones on me, or when he once again taught me things I should have already known.

Like the time I took him to get "fixed," and learned, to my horror, that "fixing" a male English springer spaniel was not (contrary to my long-held belief) a simple dog vasectomy. Of course, I didn't learn the brutal truth until the receptionist at the clinic asked us: "Pudge, for castration?"

"Not us," I nearly said aloud, trying to figure out a graceful way to retreat or vanish. Pudge looked at me bewildered, I thought. He adapted well after his surgery, but I'm quite sure he never truly forgave me.

Pudge was a bird dog by breed, but he did not know that. More correctly, my bird-hunting friends always told me, Pudge knew it innately, but was limited by an owner who didn't know how to train him.

Pudge made his debut, as I like to call it, during the Eastern Maine Sportsman's Show of 2003. He was a couple months old, stopped by to say "Hi" to me after his adoption on Friday night, and delighted thousands of show attendees for the entire weekend. The original thought was to let him "meet and greet" until he got sick of the attention. He never did.

*Gordon Doore poses with Pudge the English Springer Spaniel of John Holyoke,.
Pudge passed away in 2013, at the age of 10. Photo by Karen Holyoke.*

That night, I remember him whining in his crate, unwilling to sleep on his first night away from his mother. Eventually (desperate for him to allow me to sleep), I broke a key rule of crate training and allowed him out. He still wasn't happy and wanted attention. As would become customary, he won. I spent the night sleeping on the floor beside Pudge as he curled up in a pile of dirty clothes.

He showed a special fondness for small children, especially those in strollers. Pudge quickly learned that stroller-bound toddlers loved puppies, and whenever he saw a mom pushing a stroller, whether in a park or at an outdoors expo, he began tugging at his leash, begging to visit.

He did, however, tire of the outdoor expo grind. One spring, after a snowstorm limited travel, Pudge spent a boring Saturday morning at the Orono show waiting for a crowd that never arrived. Eventually, he showed his displeasure by cocking a leg and watering a support girder in the University of Maine field house. Point made, I took him home.

Although not a practicing bird dog, he did pay attention to birds, once in awhile. Like the time he raced out of our camp on Beech Hill Pond, vaulted down the embankment, and set out in pursuit of a dozen semi-tame ducks that had been living on a steady diet of bread thrown by local camp owners. One duck broke free from the pack, and Pudge headed after it, swimming toward open water, before a passing kayaker finally herded him back to dry land.

As a puppy he liked to drink beer, which he obtained by knocking over the bottles of visitors during cookouts and backyard parties. Later, after he started scavenging off countertops, he decided that bread was pretty tasty, a loaf at a time, thank you.

Eventually he showed promise as an amateur chef, crafting his own homemade salsa when he gobbled down five scavenged tomatoes (which I had been cultivating all summer long), and three jalapenos (ditto), eating them all in one sitting while I was away. He was still trying to train me, I suppose, although for the life of me I never thought that leaving hot peppers and tomatoes on the counter would even tempt him.

Pudge had some health woes over the years, but nothing seemed to stop him. Even when the vet sat me down and talked solemnly about tumors and cancer a few weeks back, I assumed that he'd find a way to rally. He always had.

But life doesn't work that way.

A couple days later, his time short, I called the emergency clinic and told them the bad news. I needed help. My dog needed help. Before I burst into tears, yet again, I told them I was on my way. They helped us both in ways I can never adequately express.

We had ten good years together, Pudge and I. He is still loved by Karen and me, and his two-legged adopted siblings, Mackie, Gordon, and Georgia. He is also missed, daily, by his cat-pal, Tori.

I'm left with a heavy heart and a boatload of great memories, some of which I'm grateful you've allowed me to share here. But I'm also left with this, every single day—the house doesn't sound the same any more.

And it doesn't feel the same, either.

48. Forgotten Memories

As the rest of the state alternately laments or celebrates the arrival of genuine winter weather, the Holyoke clan has headed to the mountains to renew a longstanding tradition we call "Snow Camp." It's a ski trip, of sorts, although calling it that diminishes exactly what this trip has come to mean to us.

Once a year, we all (and by all, I mean brothers and sisters, nephews, nieces, significant others and assorted pals looking to crash on a floor so that they can ski all week) head to Sugarloaf. We (and by "we," I mean my mom) rent a condo, and then we all proceed to eat too much, ski when we want to, play cutthroat games of Apples to Apples and other games, and have a ball. According to our family historians, the tradition began with my sister-in-law's family. After a few years of that, about twenty-five years ago, the Holyokes adopted the yearly trip as their own. And we've been going back every year since.

Some years, we've had more than twenty people in camp. This year, that number's a more manageable sixteen. But one camper is missing. And it hurts.

Some of you know my dad. Many times, during the outdoor expos that we staff throughout the year, I run into you, and you always ask about him. For that, I'm grateful. My dad, you see, was always a talker. Some say I've benefited from (or have been plagued by) the same chatty trait. Simply trying to walk out of a restaurant with my dad often turned into a ten-minute affair because he always saw someone he knew and stopped to chat.

He knew a lot of people. And through his work at the University of Maine, he traveled to nearly every town in Maine, it seemed, and always had a story to tell about the people who lived in Wytopitlock, Van Buren, Masardis, or Brooks.

For the second straight year, Dad isn't here with us at Snow Camp. And it's different. I'm not asking for sympathy. We're lucky, as a whole. Dad is still alive and kicking at age eighty-one. Many lose parents far too early, and we're fortunate to have so many memories to fall back on. But his memory, tragically, is another story.

My dad has Alzheimer's disease.

For the past several years, we've watched the disease slowly, inexorably, rob him of things so dear to him. Not money, nor fame. Those things never mattered much to him. Instead, he has lost his stories. And his memories. Most days, he still remembers us, although he might not use our names. But when we visit, we don't hear those funny tales about childhood pals with comical names like "Bughouse."

We talk about his past races—he was the toughest runner I ever saw, and qualified for the Boston Marathon twice on an ankle a surgeon later told him he shouldn't have been able to walk on—but to him, we're describing someone else. And like thousands of families, as he struggles with this nasty disease, we struggle, too.

Dad always lit up a room. He always had the best story, often one he shared even though it poked fun at the teller himself. He almost drowned in a manure lagoon, crashed while waterskiing and nearly cracked his head open, and mistakenly called a woman's portly dog a pig while running a road race in Camden.

Last year, Dad didn't join us at Sugarloaf. Mom and he stayed home, and she wished us well on our annual trip. Over the summer, she made the choice she dreaded most: Dad needed to stay in a facility where he could be monitored twenty-four hours a day and remain safe.

We miss him here, but we remember that for several years, the relative unfamiliarity of the condo, and being away from home, made this annual trip difficult for him. Mom is with us this year, bustling around the kitchen, watching over us all with the same firm hand we've always expected. But it's not easy for her, nor for the rest of us.

I suspect this column might resonate with many readers. That's why I chose to share it today, during one of our family's most treasured traditions. Already tonight, I've shed a few tears while trying to pen this column. I remember those old stories, the ones he told dozens of times over the years. I wish he did, too.

So as we prepare to turn the page and greet another new year, I hope you'll do me a little favor. Maybe you've got a person in your life who likes to talk. And maybe you think you're just too busy to hear another tale.

You're not.

Stop.

Listen.

Eventually, maybe at your own version of Snow Camp, you'll be glad you did.

49. A Hometown Welcome

For the past fourteen years, ever since I landed the job many have described as the best newspaper gig in the state, I've looked forward to late winter for several reasons. Among those: The melting snow signals the arrival of annual outdoor expos like the Eastern Maine Sportsmen's Show, which welcomes thousands of folks to Orono each year.

Last weekend, the first of those shows, the Penobscot Fly Fishers' Cabin Fever Reliever, took place, and as has become our custom, the *Bangor Daily News* had a great time staffing a booth at the "World Famous" Brewer Auditorium.

To be sure, the show was a return to my roots, as I spent hundreds of enjoyable hours in the building that served as the recreational hub of my hometown. And since the show moved to Brewer a number of years ago, I've come to think of the Cabin Fever Reliever as my "hometown" outdoors event, even though I no longer live in Brewer.

With that said, the Cabin Fever Reliever has still remained a professional event for me, complete with all the trappings of other outdoor shows we've staffed over the years in spots like Orono, Portland, Presque Isle, and Augusta.

The day usually looks something like this: We arrive early to set up our booth. Then we stand for most of the day, chatting with visitors about what it is that the *Bangor Daily News* is up to. We talk about our stories and listen to suggestions for potential future projects. We field criticism from those who find our pages too liberal or too conservative (yes, we hear both complaints, often within a five-minute span). We sign up folks for our "Win a Drift Boat Trip" contest, and we show them the awesome videos that my colleague, Aislinn Sarnacki, has produced.

John Holyoke takes a break from hunting in 2017, just months after suffering a series of strokes. Photo by Peter Warner.

Some of the visitors are people we know, others look familiar because we've talked to them at past shows, and still others are strangers who stop by because they're either exceedingly polite or curious, or because they share our passion for the outdoors. For the record, any of those reasons to stop and chat is OK with us.

But at this year's Cabin Fever Reliever, things felt different around the bright green *Bangor Daily News* booth. I felt it. My boss, Sarah Walker Caron, felt it. Failing to recognize what was going on, and failing to tell *Bangor Daily News* readers that we noticed, and that we appreciated their efforts, would be a major mistake.

For the better part of two days last weekend, a steady stream of show attendees stopped by our booth, just like they do every year. But this year, dozens came not to hear what we had brewing, but to share thoughts with me.

Back in December, as some of you may have read, I suffered a stroke. It was not my first (although I never knew about either of the previous two until evidence showed up on a scan of my brain). I missed a few weeks of work, came back at the first of the year, and dove back into my job.

I also tried to be as honest about my health woes as possible. To that end, while I was still in the hospital I told my boss that it would be OK if she wrote a little item for our pages, letting people know that I'd had a setback, but (and you have to read this next phrase in your best "Monty Python" accent) "I'm not dead yet."

The reasons for my honesty: I wanted folks to know that I'd be back, and I didn't want people to think that I was lying in a hospital bed, unable to move, unable to help myself.

I wanted people to know that I was lucky, and that I'd be back, perhaps not as good as ever—I've still got some tingling in my left-side extremities—but in a passable form. And I wanted to say "Thanks."

Then, last weekend, a single question kept cropping up, just as I prepared to swing into my customary *Bangor Daily News* show spiel. "How are you?" dozens of visitors asked hour after hour, sizing me up from toes to nose, just to make sure my answer confirmed their personal observations. "On the mend? How do you feel?"

Some hugged. Some offered a pat on the back or a squeeze of my arm. Nobody really cared what I had to say about the *Bangor Daily News* or our future offerings. But that was OK. They cared about me.

As the show neared its end on Sunday, I finally found a moment to consider what had just transpired and to appreciate the outpouring of support from people who share only one common trait—they read the newspaper where I've been fortunate enough to work for the past twenty-four years. Those readers have welcomed me and my peers to their breakfast tables each morning, and many have adapted to reading us on their phones or tablets over the years. And on an amazing weekend in my hometown, some of them took the time to tell me they wanted me to remain upright for a few more years.

One man, a retired teacher from my alma mater that I was never lucky enough to have had in class, grasped my arm and said a few words that I'll continue to hold close.

"Take care of yourself," he said. "I can't afford to lose another friend."

After arriving home, I found myself wishing I'd known how the weekend was going to have developed. If I had, I told myself, I would have taken a photo of every person who took the time to stop and share those kind words. Then I would have made a bulletin board on our website and said a few kind words back to each of them. Unfortunately, that idea came too late.

So I'm left with this. It might sound familiar, and I might have said something similar after I returned to work last month. Still, these closing words are all I've got.

I'm feeling fine, and continue to make progress as I become more aware of how lucky I truly am. And thank you, for your words, wishes and prayers.

I'll see you at the next show.

Acknowledgments

Over the past twenty-five years or so, I've had the good fortune of working with many folks who value the written word and who have encouraged me to head afield to find interesting stories to tell. To former *Bangor Daily News* executive editor A. Mark Woodward, who offered me the job of a lifetime, an especially heartfelt "Thanks" is in order.

To fully describe the help and inspiration all those other other wordsmiths, editors, and colleagues have offered would fill another volume. Please let this partial list suffice for now and serve as official notice that this book is ours. Not mine.

Among those important folks: Kathryn Olmstead, my advisor during a rough-and-tumble ten-year undergraduate journey through the University of Maine, for never losing faith. William "Bill" Warner for hiring me at the *Bangor Daily News* for a three-month "part-time" job, then keeping me on after that, paving the way for all kinds of fun. My section editors on the Sports and Features desks, Joe McLaughlin, Aimee Dolloff Thibodeau, and Sarah Walker Caron for pointing me in the right direction, for letting me develop my own "voice" (even when it might not fit into any stylebook we were supposed to follow), and for reeling me in when I needed it. To Aislinn Sarnacki for making our *Bangor Daily News* outdoors offerings more diverse, and for providing a strong voice to our pages. She has been a valuable creative sounding board and has helped me tell better stories that ring true to more readers. No matter their differing titles, top newsroom managers A.

Mark Woodward, Mike Dowd, Susan Young, and Anthony Ronzio for seeing the value in outdoor stories and celebrating our state's wonderful outdoor heritage and traditions. *Bangor Daily News* president Todd Benoit for allowing these tales to be shared in book form. And thanks to *Bangor Daily News* publisher Richard J. Warren for patiently allowing a new outdoors columnist to find his way.

The photographers at the *Bangor Daily News* have historically been among the company's strengths, and you've seen some of their top-notch work here. To them—Linda Coan O'Kresik, Gabor Degre, Bridget Brown, Brian Feulner and Scott Haskell, among others—it's been a pleasure to have had the chance to tell stories with you.

Pete Warner, son of Bill and Barb, my current section editor at the *Bangor Daily News*, grew up in the journalism biz, and is simply one of the best hunting and fishing buddies a guy could have. Thanks for writing this book's Foreword. And thanks for being a great friend. Chris Lander is another pal who deserves mention, for putting up with the cameras and notepads that often accompany me on our trips afield.

To the readers who've supported the *Bangor Daily News* over the years, none of these tales would have been shared without the role you played. Without a reader, the writer's successes are hollow indeed.

Thanks to my parents, Vaughn and Marjorie, for listening to all the stories I felt compelled to tell them (again and again and again), and for encouraging me to tell more. Or, perhaps, telling me to go somewhere else and tell someone who hadn't already heard those tales a few dozen times.

And to the best writer in our house, my wife Karen Holyoke, thanks for helping to make our story the best one I ever get to tell.

Bibliography

All stories published in the *Bangor Daily News* on these dates. Stories may have orginally appeared with a different title.

Prologue, The Brook, *May 26, 2005*
1. Cross Country Croquet, *August 15, 2009*
2. Hooking Up Camp Water, *June 3, 2008*
3. Camping With Kids, *June 26, 2008*
4. Time Heals Old Camping Wounds, *June 9, 2009*
5. The Everything Box, *July 22, 2010*
6. Camp Solitude, *June 6, 2006*
7. Junkapork Rock, *July 11, 2006*
8. Give 'em a Wave, *July 22, 2010*
9. Struck by Lightning, *October 12, 2002*
10. Afterword: Charles Kimball, *October 20, 2009*
11. The Jim Carter Show, *June 11, 2005*
12. Afterword: Jim Carter, *January 6, 2012*
13. A Legend Named "Wiggie," *July 16, 2005*
14. Afterword: Wiggie Robinson, *July 12, 2007*
15. "I Miss My Dad," *October 6, 2007*
16. Rescue!, *July 9, 2013*
17. Return of the Native, *August 31, 2017*
18. I Shouldn't Have Put on My Pants, *December 14, 2011*
19. Feeling Kind of Squirrelly, *August 25, 2001*
20. The Big Snip, September 17, *2011*
21. Frogzilla, *February 29, 2012*
22. How to Call Turkeys Like a Choking Cat, *May 5, 2011*
23. Setting a Trap for Ted E. Bamster, *June 23, 2008*
24. The Mighty Kenduskeag Shows No Mercy, *April 24, 2007*